simply SOUP

Kate McMillan

Photography by Erin Kunkel

**FOG
CITY**
PRESS

FOG CITY PRESS

a division of Weldon Owen Inc.
1045 Sansome Street, Suite 100, San Francisco, CA 94111
www.weldonowen.com

SIMPLY SOUP

Conceived and produced by Weldon Owen, Inc.
In collaboration with Williams-Sonoma, Inc.
3250 Van Ness Avenue, San Francisco, CA 94109

A WELDON OWEN PRODUCTION

Printed and bound in China by 1010 Printing, Ltd.

This book as been previously published as
Williams-Sonoma Soup of the Day

This edition printed in 2014
10 9 8 7 6 5 4 3 2 1

Library of Congress Cataloging-in-Publication
data is available

ISBN 13: 978-1-61628-900-3
ISBN 10: 1-61628-900-7

weldon**owen**

President Roger Shaw
Senior VP, Sales and Marketing Amy Kaneko
Finance Director Philip Paulick

Associate Publisher Amy Marr
Associate Editor Emma Rudolph

Creative Director Kelly Booth
Designer Howie Severson
Senior Production Designer Rachel Lopez Metzger

Production Director Chris Hemesath
Associate Production Director Michelle Duggan

Photographer Erin Kunkel
Food Stylist Robyn Valarik
Prop Stylist Leigh Noe

Weldon Owen is a division of **BONNIER**

ACKNOWLEDGMENTS

Weldon Owen wishes to thank the following people for their generous support in producing
this book: Donita Boles, David Bornfriend, Joe Budd, Sarah Putman Clegg, Judith Dunham,
David Evans, Alexa Hyman, Kim Laidlaw, Carolyn Miller, Julie Nelson, Jennifer Newens,
Elizabeth Parson, Hannah Rahill, Tracy White Taylor, Jason Wheeler, and Sharron Wood.

CONTENTS

A SOUP FOR EVERY DAY

Hot, cold, smooth, chunky, creamy, brothy—soups come in myriad forms, yet always delight. Considered by many to be the ultimate comfort food, they are welcome and flavorful additions to the dining table throughout the year, marking seasons and occasions with flavorful flair.

This book will inspire you to make soups on any day of the year, using what's fresh as your guide. In summer, cold soups like gazpacho are an easy no-cook solution, while hearty chicken soup provides nourishment during the winter months. For entertaining, make a big batch of wholesome soup—a meaty stew, a vegetable-laden chili, or a creamy chowder—for an instant crowd-pleaser.

Versatile, flexible, and easy to stretch, making soup is a smart way to cook. Some are perfect for casual weeknight meals, while others offer an elegant way to begin a dinner party. Soups are easy to dress up by adding texture, flavor, or a festive touch with simple garnishes—a topping of crisp garlic croutons; a swirl of pesto, olive oil, or crème fraîche; or a sprinkle of chopped fresh herbs. They are also easy to personalize to your own tastes by swapping in alternative ingredients, omitting cream or an herb you may not have on hand, or changing the texture by puréeing it or leaving it chunky. Many soups can be made ahead and reheated just before serving, while others can be prepared in large batches and frozen for quick meal options on busy nights. You'll learn these approaches and many more.

Organized by soup type, the 70 recipes in this book include suggestions for tasty variations, serving ideas, and shopping tips. There are also dozens of full-color photographs to guide and entice you along the way.

The wealth of delicious recipes, beautiful photographs, and culinary wisdom inside these pages will satisfy a yearning for soup, no matter the occasion or season.

COLD SOUPS

For a less sweet and more festive soup, replace the fruity red wine with a dry Prosecco or a sparkling rosé stirred in after chilling to preserve the bubbles. Save a little bubbly for serving alongside.

CHILLED SOUR CHERRY SOUP WITH TARRAGON

serves 6–8

3 lb (1.5 kg) fresh sour cherries, stemmed and pitted

3 Tbsp unsalted butter

4 shallots, minced

2 tsp grated lemon zest

2 cups (16 fl oz/500 ml) fruity red wine

2 Tbsp cornstarch

⅔ cup (5 oz/155 g) sugar, plus more as needed

Salt

1 lb (500 g) fresh sweet cherries, stemmed, pitted, and quartered

¼ cup (2 fl oz/60 ml) heavy cream (optional)

¼ cup (⅓ oz/10 g) chopped tarragon

Using a food processor, process the sour cherries to a smooth purée. Pour the purée through a fine-mesh sieve set over a bowl and, using a wooden spoon, press hard on the solids to extract as much liquid as possible. Discard the solids in the sieve.

In a large, heavy pot, melt the butter over medium heat. Add the shallots and sauté until softened, about 3 minutes. Stir in the lemon zest and cook until fragrant, about 45 seconds. Add the sour-cherry purée, the wine, and 1½ cups (12 fl oz/375 ml) water and stir to blend. Raise the heat to medium-high and bring to a simmer.

In a small bowl, whisk together the cornstarch with ¼ cup (2 fl oz/60 ml) water and stir it into the simmering cherry mixture along with the ⅔ cup sugar and a pinch of salt. Reduce the heat to medium-low and simmer, stirring often, until thickened to the consistency of light cream, about 4 minutes. Remove from the heat and stir in the sweet cherries. Transfer the soup to a nonaluminum bowl and let cool completely. Cover and refrigerate until well chilled, at least 4 hours or up to overnight.

When ready to serve, taste the soup and adjust the seasoning with salt and sugar. Serve, drizzled with cream, if using, and sprinkled with tarragon.

CHILLED BEET & CUCUMBER SOUP

serves 8

2 lb (1 kg) beets (about 8 beets), trimmed

1 yellow onion, quartered

8 cups (64 fl oz/2 l) chicken broth

1 Tbsp sugar

2 English cucumbers, peeled, seeded, and cut into thin strips, plus thinly sliced cucumber rounds for serving

2 Tbsp fresh lemon juice

2 Tbsp rice wine vinegar

Salt and freshly ground pepper

¼ cup (⅓ oz/10 g) finely chopped dill

1 cup (8 oz/250 g) nonfat plain yogurt or lowfat sour cream (optional)

In a large, heavy pot, combine the beets, onion, broth, 1 cup (8 fl oz/250 ml) water, and the sugar over medium-high heat. Cover and bring to a boil. Reduce the heat to low and simmer, covered, until the beets are tender, 45–60 minutes.

Using a slotted spoon, transfer the beets to a colander. Reserve the cooking liquid. Peel the beets under cold running water. Cut 3 of the beets in half. Cut the remaining beets into strips 1 inch (2.5 cm) long and ¼ inch (6 mm) wide. Cover and refrigerate the beet strips.

Strain the cooking liquid through a fine-mesh sieve into a large bowl. Remove and discard the onion. Purée the 6 beet halves and 1 cup (8 fl oz/250 ml) of the strained liquid in a food processor and add the purée to the remaining strained liquid in the bowl. Cover and refrigerate until well chilled, at least 4 hours or overnight.

Add the beet strips, cucumber strips, lemon juice, vinegar, ½ tsp salt, ¼ tsp pepper, and half of the dill to the chilled beet mixture. Stir to mix well.

Serve, garnished with the yogurt, if using, the cucumber slices, and the remaining dill.

CHILLED CUCUMBER-BUTTERMILK SOUP WITH DILLED SHRIMP

serves 4

5 English cucumbers, peeled, seeded, and chopped

4 green onions, white and tender green parts, chopped

1 large clove garlic

¼ cup (2 fl oz/60 ml) buttermilk

1½ cups (12 oz/375 g) plain whole yogurt

2 Tbsp fresh lemon juice

Salt and freshly ground pepper

FOR THE DILLED SHRIMP

¼ lb (125 g) bay shrimp, coarsely chopped

1 Tbsp chopped dill

Salt and freshly ground pepper

Put the cucumbers, green onions, and garlic into a food processor and pulse to finely chop. Add the buttermilk, yogurt, and lemon juice, and purée. Season with salt and pepper. Transfer to a covered container and refrigerate for 1 hour.

To make the dilled shrimp, put the shrimp and the dill in a small bowl and stir to combine. Season with salt and pepper.

Serve the soup, topped with the dilled shrimp.

This soup
is all about
presentation.
It'll look like
it came out of
a restaurant
kitchen, but is
surprisingly easy
to pull off. To
make the melon
strips, draw a
vegetable peeler
over a wedge of
peeled melon.

TWO MELON SOUPS

serves 4–6

FOR THE CANTALOUPE SOUP

1 very ripe cantaloupe (about 2 lb/1 kg), halved, seeded, peeled, and chopped

2 Tbsp sour cream

2 Tbsp fresh orange juice

Salt

FOR THE HONEYDEW SOUP

1 very ripe honeydew melon (about 2 lb/1 kg), halved, seeded, peeled, and chopped

2 Tbsp sour cream

2 Tbsp fresh white grape juice

Salt

Melon strips for garnish

Lime wedges for serving

To make the cantaloupe soup, purée the cantaloupe in a food processor. Add the sour cream, orange juice, and a pinch of salt and pulse several times to combine. Transfer to a covered container and refrigerate until well chilled, at least 2 hours.

Wash and dry the food processor.

To make the honeydew soup, purée the honeydew in the food processor. Add the sour cream, white grape juice, and a pinch of salt and pulse several times to combine. Transfer to a covered container and refrigerate until well chilled, at least 2 hours.

Ladle the soup into individual bowls or, to serve the soups together, put a 3-inch (7.5-cm) round cookie cutter in the center of a shallow bowl. Hold the cookie cutter in place with one hand, and with the other pour the cantaloupe soup into the center of the cookie cutter, filling it three-quarters of the way to the top. Keeping your hand on the cookie cutter, pour the honeydew soup around the outside of the cookie cutter until the bottom of the bowl is covered. Carefully lift the cookie cutter out of the bowl. Repeat for each serving. Serve, garnished with melon strips. Pass lime wedges at the table.

CHILLED CUCUMBER-YOGURT SOUP WITH LEMON & MINT

serves 8–10

6 large English cucumbers (about 5 lb/2.5 kg), peeled and seeded

8 Tbsp (¾ oz/20 g) minced mint

4 Tbsp (2 fl oz/60 ml) extra-virgin olive oil

Zest and juice of 1 large lemon

4 cups (32 fl oz/1 l) chicken broth

4 cups (2 lb/1 kg) plain yogurt

2 small cloves garlic, minced

Salt and freshly ground pepper

Finely chop 1 cucumber. Place the pieces between layers of paper towels, pressing to absorb excess moisture. Transfer to a small bowl, add 2 Tbsp of the mint and 1 Tbsp of the oil, and toss to combine. Cover and refrigerate. Cut the remaining 5 cucumbers into large chunks.

Working in batches, coarsely purée the cucumber chunks, the remaining mint, the lemon zest, and 2 cups (16 fl oz/500 ml) of the broth in a food processor or blender. Transfer to a large nonreactive bowl. Add the remaining 2 cups broth along with the finely chopped cucumber and mint mixture, the remaining 3 Tbsp oil, the lemon juice, the yogurt, and the garlic. Add 1½ tsp salt and season with pepper. Stir to blend well, cover, and refrigerate until well chilled, at least 4 hours or up to 12 hours. Serve.

CURRIED CARROT PURÉE

Here, curry powder and orange juice add flavor and vibrancy to this earthy carrot soup. To mix it up, try a touch of ground cinnamon or ginger in place of or in addition to the curry powder.

serves 4

1 Tbsp olive oil, plus more for drizzling

1 large shallot, minced

1½ lb (750 g) carrots, peeled and coarsely chopped

1 tsp curry powder

6 cups (48 fl oz/1.5 l) chicken broth

2 Tbsp fresh orange juice

Salt and freshly ground pepper

In a large, heavy pot, warm the 1 Tbsp oil over medium heat. Add the shallot and sauté until translucent, about 2 minutes. Add the carrots, curry powder, and broth. Raise the heat to medium-high and bring to a boil. Reduce the heat to low, cover, and cook until the carrots are tender, about 20 minutes. Remove from the heat and add the orange juice. Let cool slightly.

Working in batches, purée the soup in a blender or food processor. Season with salt and pepper.

The soup can be served warm or chilled. To serve warm, return to the pot and gently warm over medium heat. To serve chilled, let cool, transfer to a covered container, and refrigerate for at least 3 hours or up to overnight. Serve, drizzled with oil.

WATERMELON GAZPACHO WITH GOAT CHEESE CROÛTES

What a summertime treat to turn watermelon into a delicious and unexpected soup with a bit of a jalapeño kick. Make plenty of goat cheese croûtes and watch them vanish, as the salty cheese pairs beautifully with the sweet watermelon.

serves 6

4 cups (1½ lb/750 g) peeled and diced ripe watermelon

1 small English cucumber, peeled, seeded, and chopped

1 small ripe tomato, chopped

2 green onions, white and green parts, chopped

½ small jalapeño chile, seeded and chopped

1 tsp white wine vinegar

2 tsp extra-virgin olive oil

Salt and freshly ground pepper

FOR THE GOAT CHEESE CROÛTES

3 oz (90 g) goat cheese, at room temperature

2 Tbsp heavy cream

1 small and thin sweet baguette, thinly sliced

Put 3 cups (18 oz/560 g) of the watermelon into a food processor and pulse several times to coarsely chop, but not purée, the watermelon. Transfer to a bowl. Using a chef's knife, finely dice the remaining 1 cup (6 oz/185 g) watermelon and add to the bowl with the processed watermelon. The mixture should be very chunky.

Put the cucumber, tomato, green onions, and jalapeño into the food processor and purée. Transfer the purée to the bowl with the watermelon. Stir in the vinegar and oil. Season with salt and pepper. Cover the bowl and refrigerate for 1 hour.

To make the goat cheese croûtes, preheat the broiler to high. Put the goat cheese and cream into a bowl and stir to combine. Season with salt and pepper. Spread a thick layer of the goat cheese onto the baguette slices. Transfer to a baking sheet and put under the broiler until the cheese melts and turns golden, 2–3 minutes.

Serve the soup, and pass the goat cheese croûtes at the table.

VEGETABLE SOUPS

RED CABBAGE & APPLE SOUP

serves 4

4 Golden Delicious apples, about 1 lb (500 g) total

2 Tbsp unsalted butter

1 yellow onion, minced

1 head red cabbage, about ¾ lb (375 g), cored and very thinly sliced

¼ cup (2 fl oz/60 ml) red wine vinegar

4½ cups (36 fl oz/1.1 l) beef broth

Salt and freshly ground pepper

2 tsp fresh lemon juice

⅓ cup (3 oz/80 g) sour cream (optional)

¼ cup (⅓ oz/10 g) chopped dill

Leaving them unpeeled, cut 2 of the apples into quarters, core them, and then cut into 1-inch (2.5-cm) cubes. Set aside.

In a large, heavy pot, melt the butter over medium heat. When it is foaming, add the onion and sauté until translucent, 2–3 minutes. Add the apple cubes and sauté until softened slightly, 3–4 minutes. Add the cabbage and sauté, stirring often, until it glistens and the color has lightened, 5–6 minutes. Add the vinegar and bring to a simmer, stirring to scrape up any browned bits on the pan bottom. Add the broth, ½ tsp salt, and ½ tsp pepper and bring to a boil over medium-high heat. Reduce the heat to low, cover, and simmer until the cabbage and apples are tender, about 15 minutes.

While the soup is simmering, peel, halve, and core the remaining 2 apples, then shred them finely on a box grater. Place in a small bowl, add the lemon juice, and toss to coat. Set aside.

When the soup is ready, remove from the heat and stir in three-fourths of the shredded apples. Serve, topped with sour cream, if using, and sprinkled with the remaining shredded apples and the dill.

Southwestern ingredients mingle in this surprisingly light chowder. It gets its creamy consistency not from dairy but by puréeing half of the soup. Serve with fresh tortilla chips and salsa.

SWEET POTATO–CORN CHOWDER WITH AVOCADO

serves 6

2 Tbsp olive oil

1 small white onion, finely diced

2 cloves garlic, minced

2 tsp ground cumin

½ tsp ground coriander

Salt and freshly ground pepper

2 sweet potatoes (about 1½ lb/750 g total), peeled and diced

3 cups (24 fl oz/750 ml) vegetable or chicken broth

1 red bell pepper, seeded and finely diced

8 ears fresh corn, husks and silk removed and kernels cut from cobs, or 3½ cups (1 lb/500 g) thawed frozen corn kernels

2 Tbsp minced cilantro

1 ripe avocado, pitted, peeled, and diced

½ cup (4 oz/125 g) sour cream (optional)

In a large, heavy pot, warm the oil over medium-high heat. Add the onion and garlic and sauté until translucent, about 5 minutes. Add the cumin, coriander, and salt and pepper to taste and cook for 1 minute. Add the sweet potatoes, stir to coat, and cook for 3 minutes.

Add the broth, bring to a boil, and reduce the heat to low. Simmer until the sweet potatoes are tender, about 20 minutes. Add the red pepper and corn and cook until the vegetables are tender, 10 minutes. Remove from the heat and let cool slightly.

Purée half of the soup in a blender. Return to the pot. Stir in the cilantro and season with salt and pepper. Serve, garnished with the avocado and the sour cream, if desired.

RIBOLLITA

serves 6–8

½ cup (4 fl oz/125 ml) extra-virgin olive oil,
plus more for serving

2 carrots, peeled and coarsely chopped

2 celery stalks, chopped

2 yellow onions, coarsely chopped

2 potatoes, peeled and cut into chunks

2 zucchini, coarsely chopped

1 cup (6 oz/185 g) canned diced tomatoes

1 bunch Tuscan kale (lacinato kale), tough center stalks removed,
leaves cut into thick strips

½ head savoy cabbage, coarsely chopped

1 bunch spinach, stemmed and coarsely chopped

1½ cans (21 oz/655 g) cannellini or other white beans, drained

Leaves from 3 thyme sprigs

Salt and freshly ground pepper

5 slices day-old country-style bread, toasted

In a large, heavy pot over medium heat, warm the ½ cup oil. Add the carrots, celery, onions, potatoes, and zucchini and sauté until the vegetables are softened, 10–15 minutes. Stir in the tomatoes with their juices and 4 cups (32 fl oz/1 l) water, then add the kale, cabbage, and spinach. Raise the heat to high, bring to a simmer, reduce the heat to low, and let cook until the greens are tender, about 45 minutes.

Stir in the beans and cook over medium heat for 10 minutes. Add the thyme leaves and season with salt and pepper. Remove from the heat and let cool, then cover and refrigerate overnight.

The following day, preheat the oven to 350°F (180°C). Line a 2-qt (2-l) baking dish with the toasted bread slices and ladle the soup over the top. Bake, stirring occasionally with a wooden spoon so that the bread slices break apart and blend with the soup, 20–25 minutes. Continue baking without stirring until a lightly browned crust forms on top of the soup, 5–10 minutes longer.

Season generously with oil and freshly ground pepper and serve.

TUSCAN FARRO SOUP WITH WHITE BEANS, TOMATOES & BASIL

serves 6

½ cup (3 oz/90 g) farro

Salt and freshly ground pepper

3 Tbsp olive oil

1 large yellow onion, chopped

3 cloves garlic, minced

4 cups (32 fl oz/1 l) chicken broth

1 can (15 oz/470 g) cannellini or other white beans, drained

1 can (14½ oz/455 g) diced tomatoes

2 cups packed (2½ oz/75 g) baby spinach

½ cup (¾ oz/20 g) chopped basil

In a small saucepan, bring 1½ cups (12 fl oz/375 ml) water to a boil. Add the farro and a pinch of salt, reduce the heat to low, and cook, partially covered, until all the water is absorbed, 20–25 minutes.

In a large, heavy pot, warm the oil over medium-high heat. Add the onion and garlic and sauté until translucent, about 5 minutes. Add the broth and bring to a boil. Reduce the heat to low and add the beans, tomatoes with their juices, and farro. Bring to a simmer and cook, uncovered, for 10 minutes to blend the flavors. Add the spinach and basil and stir just until the spinach is wilted. Season with salt and pepper and serve.

TOMATO, ZUCCHINI & FRESH CORN SOUP

serves 4–6

2 zucchini, trimmed, halved, and sliced

3 Tbsp olive oil

Salt and freshly ground pepper

1 yellow onion, chopped

5 cloves garlic, minced

4 plum tomatoes, chopped

4 cups (32 fl oz/1 l) vegetable or chicken broth

1 cup (6 oz/180 g) corn kernels (from about 2 ears)

⅓ cup (½ oz/15 g) chopped basil

Preheat the oven to 400°F (200°C). Toss the zucchini with 1 Tbsp of the oil and season with salt and pepper. Spread on a baking sheet and roast for 20 minutes. Set aside.

In a large, heavy pot, warm the remaining 2 Tbsp oil over medium-high heat. Add the onion and garlic and sauté until soft, about 5 minutes. Add the tomatoes, stir to combine, and cook for 3 minutes. Add the broth and bring to a boil. Reduce the heat to low and simmer for 20 minutes. Remove from the heat and let cool slightly.

Purée half of the soup in a blender. Return to the pot and season with salt and pepper. Return the soup to a boil, add the corn, and cook for 5 minutes. Add the zucchini and stir in the basil. Serve.

CHUNKY HEIRLOOM TOMATO & BASIL SOUP

Combining red and yellow tomatoes gives this soup a beautiful color. Keep the soup chunky, because when tomatoes are in season you really want to let their texture shine. Serve with bread sticks and butter or garlic croutons.

serves 6

3 Tbsp olive oil

1 large yellow onion, chopped

4 cloves garlic, minced

2 carrots, peeled and finely chopped

3 red heirloom tomatoes (about 2 lb/1 kg total), coarsely chopped

3 yellow heirloom tomatoes (about 2 lb/1 kg total), coarsely chopped

2 cups (16 fl oz/500 ml) chicken broth

2 tsp sugar

1 Tbsp heavy cream

⅓ cup (⅓ oz/10 g) chopped basil

Salt and freshly ground pepper

In a large, heavy pot, warm the oil over medium-high heat. Add the onion, garlic, and carrots and sauté until very soft, about 5 minutes. Add the tomatoes, broth, and sugar, stirring to combine, and bring to a boil. Reduce the heat to low and simmer for 30 minutes. Remove from the heat and let cool slightly.

Transfer half of the soup to a food processor and purée. Return to the pot and add the cream. Stir in the basil, season to taste with salt and pepper, and serve.

SPINACH & VERMICELLI SOUP WITH FRIED EGG

serves 4

1 Tbsp olive oil

½ small yellow onion, thinly sliced

1 clove garlic, minced

5 cups (40 fl oz/1.25 l) chicken broth

½ lb (250 g) vermicelli, broken into 2-inch (5-cm) pieces

1 bunch spinach, stemmed

1 Tbsp unsalted butter

4 eggs

Hot sauce, such as Sriracha, for serving (optional)

In a large saucepan, warm the oil over medium-high heat. Add the onion and garlic and sauté until translucent, about 5 minutes. Add the broth and bring to a boil. Add the vermicelli, return to a boil, and cook, stirring occasionally, for 4 minutes. Add the spinach and stir through just until it is wilted, about 2 minutes. Reduce the heat to low to keep the soup warm while you prepare the eggs.

In a nonstick frying pan, melt the butter over medium heat. Fry each egg until it is set but the yolk is still runny, 5–6 minutes.

Ladle the soup into bowls and top each with a fried egg. Serve, passing the hot sauce at the table, if using.

PINTO BEAN SOUP WITH TOASTED JALAPEÑOS

Toasting fresh chiles and garlic on the stove top until they're charred and blistered deepens and mellows their strong flavors, coaxing out a subtle sweetness and adding a suggestion of smokiness to dishes like this soup.

serves 6–8

6 cups (48 fl oz/1.5 l) chicken broth

1 smoked ham hock

6 jalapeño chiles

4 cloves garlic

2 Tbsp olive oil

2 yellow onions, finely chopped

2 carrots, peeled and finely chopped

1½ tsp dried oregano

1½ tsp ground cumin

¾ tsp ground coriander

¾ tsp chili powder

1 can (14½ oz/455 g) diced tomatoes

2 cans (14½ oz/455 g each) pinto beans, drained

¼ cup (2 fl oz/60 ml) fresh lime juice

Salt and freshly ground pepper

1 cup (8 oz/250 g) sour cream

⅓ cup (⅓ oz/10 g) cilantro leaves

In a large saucepan, bring the broth and ham hock to a boil over medium-high heat. Reduce the heat to low, cover, and simmer until fragrant, 1 hour. Discard the ham hock.

Meanwhile, in a small frying pan, toast the jalapeños and garlic over medium heat, tossing occasionally, until lightly charred, about 15 minutes. Let cool. Seed and mince 4 of the chiles. Cut the remaining 2 chiles into thin rings. Mince the garlic.

In a large, heavy pot, warm the oil over medium heat. Add the onions and carrots and sauté until softened, about 6 minutes. Stir in the minced chiles, garlic, oregano, cumin, coriander, and chili powder and sauté until fragrant, about 2 minutes. Add the ham broth, tomatoes with their juices, and beans. Bring to a boil, reduce the heat to low, and simmer for 20 minutes to blend the flavors. Remove from the heat and let cool slightly.

Working in batches, purée half of the soup in a blender. Return to the pot. Add the lime juice, 2½ tsp salt, and pepper to taste. Reheat over medium-low heat, stirring occasionally, for 10 minutes. Serve, garnished with the sour cream, toasted jalapeño rings, and cilantro.

To make pistou, in a blender, combine 3–4 cloves garlic, ¼ teaspoon coarse sea salt, 1 cup (1 oz/30 g) basil leaves and process until a paste forms. With the motor running, add ⅓ cup (3 fl oz/ 80 ml) extra-virgin olive oil in a slow, steady stream, processing until the mixture is thick and green. Refrigerate in an airtight container for up to 5 days. Makes ½ cup (4 fl oz/125 ml).

PROVENÇAL MINESTRONE

serves 4–6

2 cups (16 fl oz/500 ml) chicken broth

3 small boiling potatoes, peeled and diced

2 carrots, peeled and diced

1 tsp fresh thyme leaves, or ½ tsp dried

1 tsp minced fresh winter savory, or ½ tsp dried

Salt and freshly ground pepper

1 large zucchini, diced

1 small yellow onion, diced

½ lb (250 g) young, slender green beans, trimmed and cut into 1-inch (2.5-cm) pieces

1 lb (500 g) fresh cranberry beans in the pod, shelled, or 1 cup (7 oz/220 g) canned butter beans

½ cup (3 oz/90 g) spaghetti broken into 2-inch (5-cm) pieces

Pistou *(left)*

In a large, heavy pot, bring the broth and 6 cups (48 fl oz/1.5 l) water to a boil over medium-high heat. Add the potatoes, carrots, thyme, winter savory, 2 tsp salt, and ½ tsp pepper. Reduce the heat to medium and cook until the carrots are tender when pierced with a fork, about 20 minutes.

Add the zucchini, onion, green beans, and shelling beans and cook until the shelling beans are tender to the bite, 15–20 minutes.

Add the spaghetti and cook until al dente, 10–11 minutes, or according to the package directions. Taste and adjust the seasoning. Stir 2 Tbsp of the pistou into the soup.

Ladle the soup into bowls and serve, passing the remaining pistou at the table.

This soup can also be served smooth: after cooking the vegetables, purée them in batches in a blender. The charred eggplant turns silky and almost creamy, and the pleasant smoky flavor pervades the soup.

CHARRED EGGPLANT SOUP WITH CUMIN & GREEK YOGURT

serves 6–8

1 Tbsp olive oil, plus more for brushing

2 large eggplants (about 2½ lb/1.25 kg total), peeled and cut crosswise into slices 1 inch (2.5 cm) thick

3 ripe tomatoes (about 1¼ lb/625 g total), cored, halved, and seeded

3 carrots, peeled and finely chopped

5 shallots, finely chopped

3 cloves garlic, minced

¾ tsp minced thyme

¼ tsp ground cumin

1 cup (8 fl oz/250 ml) dry white wine

5 cups (40 fl oz/1.25 l) chicken or vegetable broth

Salt and freshly ground pepper

½ cup (4 oz/125 g) Greek-style plain yogurt (optional)

Prepare a charcoal or gas grill for direct-heat cooking over medium-high heat. Brush the grate with oil. Brush the eggplant slices and tomato halves with oil and arrange on the grill directly over the heat. Cook, turning as needed, until softened and nicely grill-marked, about 8 minutes for the tomatoes and 10 minutes for the eggplant. Transfer to a cutting board. When cool enough to handle, peel and discard the skins from the tomatoes. Coarsely chop the eggplant slices.

In a large, heavy pot, warm the 1 Tbsp oil over medium-high heat. Add the carrots and sauté until just beginning to soften, about 4 minutes. Add the shallots, garlic, thyme, and cumin and cook, stirring occasionally, until fragrant, about 2 minutes. Add the tomatoes, chopped eggplant, wine, and broth and bring to a boil. Reduce the heat to low, cover partially, and simmer for 20 minutes to blend the flavors. Season with 1½ tsp salt and pepper to taste. Serve, garnished with a dollop of yogurt, if using.

CHEESE & ARUGULA RAVIOLI SOUP

serves 4

FOR THE RAVIOLI

1 tsp olive oil

½ cup (½ oz/15 g) arugula

⅓ cup (3 oz/90 g) ricotta cheese

2 Tbsp grated Parmesan cheese

Pinch of grated nutmeg

Salt and freshly ground pepper

20 wonton wrappers

2 Tbsp olive oil

2 shallots, thinly sliced

4 cloves garlic, thinly sliced

4 cups (32 fl oz/1 l) chicken broth

1 can (14½ oz/455 g) diced tomatoes

1 Tbsp tomato paste

Salt and freshly ground pepper

1 cup (1 oz/30 g) arugula

¼ cup (⅓ oz/10 g) chopped basil

Grated Parmesan cheese for garnish

To make the ravioli, warm the oil in a small frying pan over medium heat. Add the arugula and sauté until wilted, 1 minute. Transfer the arugula to a cutting board, let cool slightly, and finely chop.

In a small bowl, combine the ricotta, Parmesan, nutmeg, and chopped arugula and season with salt and pepper. Place 1 tsp of the cheese mixture in the middle of each wonton wrapper. Moisten all sides of a wrapper with water and fold the wrapper diagonally, forcing out air bubbles as you press to seal. Repeat for all the ravioli.

To make the soup, in a large, heavy pot, warm the oil over medium-high heat. Add the shallots and garlic and cook until soft, about 4 minutes. Add the broth, tomatoes, and tomato paste and bring to a boil. Reduce the heat to low and simmer for 10 minutes. Season with salt and pepper.

Return the soup to a gentle boil. Carefully add the ravioli and cook for about 2 minutes. Add the arugula and basil and cook just until the greens are wilted, about 1 minute. Serve, passing Parmesan at the table.

ARTICHOKE & QUINOA SOUP WITH GREEN GARLIC

The fresh, mellow flavor of green garlic adds a welcome springtime accent in this earthy soup that combines nutty quinoa and sweet, mild-tasting artichokes. You can substitute cooked barley or farro for the quinoa.

serves 6–8

Juice of ½ lemon

12 artichokes

2 Tbsp unsalted butter

1 yellow onion, finely diced

4 heads green garlic, white and pale green bottoms finely chopped, tender green tops thinly sliced

½ tsp minced thyme

6 cups (48 fl oz/1.5 l) chicken broth

¾ cup (8 oz/250 g) quinoa, cooked

Salt and freshly ground pepper

Extra-virgin olive oil for serving

Fill a large bowl with water and add the lemon juice. Cut off the stem of each artichoke flush with the bottom. Snap off the outer leaves until you reach the tender inner leaves. Cut off the top one-third of the artichoke. As you work, add the artichokes to the lemon water.

In a large pot fitted with a steamer basket, bring 2–3 inches (5–7.5 cm) of water to a boil over medium-high heat. Place the artichokes in the steamer. Cover and cook until the bottoms are tender when pierced with a knife, 35–40 minutes. Drain upside down on paper towels until cool. Pull off the leaves from each artichoke and cut out the chokes. Finely chop the hearts.

In a large, heavy pot, melt the butter over medium heat. Add the onion and sauté until softened, about 5 minutes. Add the chopped green garlic bottoms and cook until fragrant, 3–4 minutes. Add the thyme, broth, and chopped artichokes, raise the heat to high, and bring to a boil. Reduce the heat to low, cover, and simmer for about 10 minutes to blend the flavors.

Purée half of the mixture in a blender and return to the pot. Add the quinoa and 1½ tsp salt, and season with pepper. Cook gently over medium-low heat until heated through, about 10 minutes. Ladle the soup into bowls and drizzle with olive oil. Sprinkle with pepper and the green garlic tops and serve.

To make the fried rosemary, in a small frying pan, warm 2 Tbsp olive oil over high heat. Add 4 sprigs rosemary, 2 at a time, and fry for 1 minute on each side. Transfer to paper towels to drain. Once they are cool enough to handle, remove the leaves and chop, if desired.

CHICKPEA & ROASTED TOMATO SOUP WITH FRIED ROSEMARY

serves 4–6

1 lb (500 g) Roma (plum) tomatoes

4 Tbsp olive oil

Salt and freshly ground pepper

1 large yellow onion, chopped

4 cloves garlic, minced

1 tsp ground cumin

½ tsp paprika

1 cinnamon stick

3 cans (15 oz/470 g each) chickpeas, drained

4 cups (32 fl oz/1 l) chicken broth

1 Tbsp sour cream

Fried Rosemary for garnish *(left)*

Preheat the oven to 450°F (230°C). Slice the tomatoes in half and place in a single layer on a baking sheet. Drizzle with 2 Tbsp of the oil and season with salt and pepper. Roast the tomatoes until they are soft and caramelized, 25–30 minutes. Set aside.

In a large, heavy pot, warm 2 Tbsp oil over medium-high heat. Add the onion and the garlic and sauté until soft, about 5 minutes. Add the cumin, paprika, and cinnamon stick and toast the spices, stirring often, for 2 minutes. Add the chickpeas, roasted tomatoes, and broth, stir to combine, and bring to a boil. Reduce the heat to low and simmer until the chickpeas are very tender, about 45 minutes. Remove from the heat and let cool slightly.

Transfer about two-thirds of the chickpeas and broth to a blender and purée. Return to the pot and stir in the sour cream.

Season the soup with salt and pepper and serve, garnished with fried rosemary.

ARTICHOKE, SPRING PEA & MINT SOUP

serves 4–6

Juice of ½ lemon

12 small artichokes

2 Tbsp unsalted butter

1 yellow onion, finely chopped

2 cloves garlic, minced

½ lb (250 g) cremini mushrooms, thinly sliced

5 cups (40 fl oz/1.25 l) chicken broth

1 cup (5 oz/155 g) fresh peas

2 Tbsp chopped mint

Salt and freshly ground pepper

Fill a bowl with water and add the lemon juice. Cut off the stem of each artichoke flush with the bottom. Snap off the outer leaves until you reach the tender inner leaves. Cut off the top one-third of each artichoke to remove the pointed tips. Quarter the artichoke lengthwise. Cut out the choke from each quarter. As you work, add the quarters to the lemon water.

In a large, heavy pot, melt the butter over medium heat. Add the onion and garlic and cook until translucent, about 5 minutes. Drain the artichoke quarters and add to the pan with the mushrooms. Stir to coat, and cook for 4 minutes. Add the broth and bring to a boil. Reduce the heat to low and simmer, uncovered, until the artichokes are tender but not mushy, about 10 minutes. Add the peas and cook for 3 minutes. Stir in the mint, season with salt and pepper, and serve.

To make the
meyer lemon
crème fraîche,
in a small bowl,
combine ½ cup
(4 oz/125 g)
room-temperature
crème fraîche
or sour cream;
the grated zest
of 1 Meyer lemon;
1 Tbsp fresh
Meyer lemon
juice; and a
pinch of salt.

BLACK BEAN SOUP WITH MEYER LEMON CRÈME FRAÎCHE

serves 4–6

½ lb (250 g) dried black beans, picked over and rinsed

1 Tbsp olive oil

1 small white onion, chopped

2 cloves garlic, minced

1 small jalapeño chile, seeded and minced

1 tsp ground cumin

¼ cup (2 fl oz/60 ml) dry sherry

4 cups (32 fl oz/1 l) chicken or vegetable broth

Salt and freshly ground pepper

Meyer Lemon Crème Fraîche *(left)*

2 green onions, dark and light green parts only,
sliced (optional)

Place the dried beans in a bowl with cold water to cover and soak for at least 4 hours or up to overnight. Drain.

In a large, heavy pot, warm the oil over medium-high heat. Add the onion and garlic and sauté until softened, about 5 minutes. Add the jalapeño and cumin and cook, stirring constantly, for 2 minutes. Add the beans, sherry, and broth and bring to a boil. Reduce the heat to low and simmer, covered, until the beans are tender, about 1¼ hours.

For a smooth soup, remove the pot from the heat and let cool slightly. Working in batches, purée the soup in a blender. Return to the pot and warm over low heat. Season with salt and pepper.

Top the soup with the crème fraîche and green onions, if using, and serve.

PARMESAN STRACIATELLA WITH KALE

Just a few elements make up this simple soup, so use only the finest-quality ingredients you can find, like rich chicken broth, farm-fresh eggs, and freshly grated Parmigiano-Reggiano cheese. Spinach can be substituted for the kale.

serves 6–8

8 cups (64 fl oz/2 l) chicken broth

1 bunch kale, thick stems and ribs removed, roughly torn

1 tsp cornstarch

5 eggs

Salt and freshly ground pepper

1 cup (4 oz/125 g) grated Parmesan cheese

2 Tbsp extra-virgin olive oil

In a large saucepan, bring the broth to a simmer over medium-high heat. Divide the kale among bowls.

In a bowl, mix together the cornstarch and 2 tsp water. Add the eggs, season with salt and pepper, and whisk to blend.

Stir two-thirds of the cheese and the oil into the broth. Stir the egg mixture and drizzle into the broth in a circular motion. Stir gently so that the egg forms thin ribbons. Remove from the heat and let stand until the eggs are cooked through, about 1½ minutes. Ladle the broth over the kale and serve, passing the remaining cheese at the table.

Every ingredient
in this warming
peasant-style
soup, from the
chickpeas and
fresh herbs to the
farro and porcini
mushrooms,
invokes Tuscany.
For the most
authentic pairing,
serve with a
Chianti Classico.

CHICKPEA, PORCINI & FARRO SOUP

serves 4–6

1½ cups (9½ oz/295 g) dried chickpeas, picked over and rinsed

⅓ cup (3 fl oz/80 ml) olive oil

1 yellow onion, finely chopped

2 cloves garlic, minced

1 small rosemary sprig

1 Tbsp tomato paste

Salt and freshly ground pepper

4 cups (32 fl oz/1 l) vegetable broth or water

⅓ cup (2 oz/60 g) farro

FOR THE MUSHROOMS

½ lb (250 g) porcini or cremini mushrooms

1½ Tbsp extra-virgin olive oil

1 clove garlic, minced

2 Tbsp dry white wine

1 thyme sprig

Salt and freshly ground pepper

1½ tsp unsalted butter

Extra-virgin olive oil for drizzling

Put the chickpeas in a large bowl with water to cover and soak for at least 4 hours or up to overnight. Drain the chickpeas, rinse well, and place in a large saucepan. Add 8 cups (64 fl oz/2 l) cold water and bring to a boil over high heat. Reduce the heat to low and simmer, uncovered, until the chickpeas are tender, about 2 hours.

In a large, heavy pot, warm the oil over medium-low heat. Add the onion, garlic, and rosemary and sauté until the onion is softened, 5–7 minutes. In a small bowl, dissolve the tomato paste in 1 cup (8 fl oz/250 ml) warm water, and add to the pot. Stir in the chickpeas and their cooking liquid and season with salt and pepper. Bring to a simmer over medium heat and cook for 3 minutes. Add the broth, return to a simmer, and cook, uncovered, until the flavors have blended, about 30 minutes. Remove from the heat and let cool slightly. Discard the rosemary sprig.

Working in batches, purée the soup in a blender. Return to the pot and bring to a simmer over medium heat. Add the farro and cook until tender yet still slightly chewy, about 25 minutes.

Meanwhile, to prepare the mushrooms, thinly slice them lengthwise. In a large frying pan, warm the oil over medium heat. Add the garlic and sauté until fragrant, about 1 minute. Add the mushrooms and cook, stirring, until they begin to soften, 3–4 minutes. Raise the heat to high, add the wine and thyme, and cook, stirring constantly, for about 3 minutes. Reduce the heat to low, season with salt and pepper, and continue to cook, stirring often, until the mushroom juices have evaporated, about 15 minutes. Remove from the heat and discard the thyme sprig. Stir in the butter.

Stir the mushrooms into the soup. Serve, drizzled with olive oil and garnished with a grinding of pepper.

For easy variations, substitute other small filled pasta, such as ravioli, or use Swiss chard or spinach in place of the escarole.

TORTELLINI & ESCAROLE SOUP

serves 6

6 cups (48 fl oz/1.5 l) chicken broth

8 oz (250 g) fresh tortellini

1 small head escarole (6–8 oz/185–250 g)

Salt and freshly ground pepper

¾ cup (3 oz/90 g) grated Parmesan cheese

In a large, heavy pot, bring the broth and 2 cups (16 fl oz/500 ml) water to a boil over medium-high heat. Reduce the heat to medium, add the tortellini, cover, and cook until al dente, 4–5 minutes, or according to the package directions.

Meanwhile, cut the core end from the escarole. Remove the leaves from the head, rinse, and dry well. Pile the leaves on top of one another and cut into ¼-inch (6-mm) strips.

When the tortellini are done, add the escarole and season with salt and pepper. Simmer, uncovered, until the escarole is soft, about 2 minutes. Serve, garnished with the Parmesan.

TURKEY-NOODLE SOUP WITH SPINACH

A noodle soup is the perfect way to finish off the last bits of meat from a turkey roast. If you just can't take one more day of the bird, stick this in your freezer and save it for another time.

serves 8–10

2 Tbsp olive oil

1 yellow onion, chopped

3 cloves garlic, minced

3 carrots, peeled and finely diced

4 celery ribs, finely diced

1½ Tbsp minced thyme

8 cups (64 fl oz/2 l) chicken broth

½ lb (250 g) wide egg noodles

2½ cups (15 oz/470 g) shredded cooked turkey meat

2 cups (2 oz/60 g) packed spinach leaves

Salt and freshly ground pepper

In a large, heavy pot, warm the oil over medium-high heat. Add the onion, garlic, carrots, celery, and thyme and sauté until the carrots begin to soften, about 8 minutes. Add the broth and bring to a boil. Add the egg noodles and cook until al dente, about 5 minutes. Add the turkey and spinach and stir to combine. Simmer the soup for 5 minutes to blend the flavors. Season to taste with salt and pepper and serve.

CREAM SOUPS

KUMQUAT-CARROT PURÉE WITH TOASTED FENNEL SEEDS

serves 4

2 tsp fennel seeds

4 Tbsp (2 oz/60 g) unsalted butter

1 small yellow onion, chopped

2 cloves garlic, minced

1 cup kumquats, unpeeled, chopped, plus kumquat slices for garnish

2 lb (1 kg) carrots, peeled and thinly sliced

5 cups (40 fl oz/1.25 l) chicken broth

Salt and freshly ground pepper

In a small frying pan, toast the fennel seeds over medium heat just until fragrant, about 3 minutes. Transfer to a spice grinder and grind finely.

In a large, heavy pot, melt the butter over medium-high heat. Add the onion and garlic and sauté until translucent, about 5 minutes. Add the kumquats and carrots and sauté for 10 minutes. Add the broth and bring to a boil. Reduce the heat to low and simmer, uncovered, until the carrots and kumquats are very soft, 35–40 minutes. Remove from the heat and let cool slightly.

Working in batches, purée the soup in a blender. Return to the pot and stir in the ground fennel. Season with salt and pepper and serve, garnished with kumquat slices.

CREAMY CAULIFLOWER SOUP WITH CRISPY PROSCIUTTO

*Be careful not
to over-salt
the soup, as
the prosciutto
garnish will add
a good amount
of salt. To make
it vegetarian, use
vegetable broth
in place of the
chicken broth
and crispy fried
shallots (page 82)
for the prosciutto.*

serves 4–6

2 oz (60 g) thinly sliced prosciutto

2 Tbsp unsalted butter

1 yellow onion, chopped

2 celery ribs, chopped

2 cloves garlic, minced

1 head cauliflower (about 1¾ lb/875 g), coarsely chopped (about 4 cups)

¼ tsp freshly grated nutmeg

4 cups (36 fl oz/1 l) chicken broth, plus more as needed

¼ cup (2 fl oz/60 ml) heavy cream

Salt and ground white pepper

Preheat the oven to 375°F (190°C). Place the prosciutto slices in a single layer on a baking sheet. Bake until crispy, 15–18 minutes. Let cool, then crumble.

In a large, heavy pot, melt the butter over medium-high heat. Add the onion, celery, and garlic and sauté until soft, 5–7 minutes. Add the cauliflower and nutmeg, stir well to coat, and cook for 5 minutes. Add the 4 cups broth and bring to a boil. Reduce the heat to low and simmer until the cauliflower is very tender, 20–25 minutes. Remove from the heat and let cool slightly.

Working in batches, purée the soup in a blender. Return to the pot and add more broth if the soup is too thick. Stir in the cream. Return the soup just to a boil, season with salt and pepper, and serve, garnished with the prosciutto.

BROCCOLI SOUP WITH PARMESAN-LEMON FRICO

This recipe uses all of the broccoli: the florets (where most of the nutrition is) and the stems (filled with fiber). Make extra frico and store in an airtight container for up to 5 days. The frico makes a delicious appetizer on its own.

serves 4–6

2 Tbsp olive oil

1 small yellow onion, chopped

3 cloves garlic, minced

1 large bunch broccoli, cut into small florets, stems peeled and coarsely chopped

3 cups (24 fl oz/750 ml) chicken broth

½ cup (4 fl oz/125 ml) heavy cream

Salt and freshly ground pepper

FOR THE PARMESAN-LEMON FRICO

½ cup (2 oz/60 g) grated Parmesan cheese

2 tsp grated lemon zest

In a large, heavy pot, warm the oil over medium-high heat. Add the onion and garlic and sauté until very soft, about 5 minutes. Add the broccoli, stir, and cook for about 2 minutes. Add 2 cups (16 fl oz/500 ml) of the broth, cover, and cook for 6 minutes. Remove from the heat and let cool slightly.

Working in batches, purée the soup in a blender or food processor with the remaining 1 cup (8 fl oz/250 ml) broth. Return to the pot and stir in the cream. Return the soup to a gentle boil and cook for 2 minutes. Season with salt and pepper. Keep warm over low heat.

To make the Parmesan-lemon frico, preheat the oven to 400°F (200°C) and line a baking sheet with parchment paper. In a small bowl, stir together the Parmesan and lemon zest. Transfer a heaping teaspoonful of the cheese mixture onto the prepared baking sheet and use your fingers to flatten the mound. Repeat with the remaining cheese mixture, placing the mounds 1 inch (2.5 cm) apart. Bake the frico until golden brown, 3–5 minutes. Let cool on the baking sheet, then carefully lift using a spatula.

Ladle the soup into bowls, top each with 2 frico, and serve.

Classic tomato soup gets a punch with smoked paprika and crumbled bacon. Serve with savory panini, such as provolone and arugula or Cheddar and sage.

TOMATO SOUP WITH SMOKED PAPRIKA & BACON

serves 4–6

4 slices thick-cut bacon

1 Tbsp unsalted butter

1 yellow onion, chopped

2 cloves garlic, minced

2 cans (28 oz/875 g each) crushed tomatoes

3 Tbsp heavy cream

1¼ tsp smoked paprika

Salt and freshly ground pepper

In a large, heavy saucepan, fry the bacon over medium heat, turning once, until crispy, 8–10 minutes. Transfer to paper towels. Let cool, then crumble.

Add the butter to the pan and melt over medium heat. Add the onion and garlic and sauté until very soft, about 5 minutes. Add the tomatoes and bring to a boil. Reduce the heat to low and simmer for 20 minutes. Remove from the heat and let cool slightly.

Working in batches, purée the soup in a blender. Return to the saucepan and add the cream, paprika, and ½ tsp salt. Return just to a boil, turn off the heat, taste, and adjust the seasoning.

Serve, topped with the crumbled bacon and a generous grinding of pepper.

PUMPKIN SOUP WITH SPICY PUMPKIN SEEDS

The best part about this recipe is that it uses almost the entire pumpkin, and the seeds from the pumpkin are roasted to use for the garnish. Pack leftover toasted pumpkin seeds in your child's lunchbox for a fun treat.

serves 6

1 small pumpkin (about 3 lb/1.5 kg), such as Sugar Pie, peeled, seeded, and chopped

2 Tbsp olive oil

Salt and freshly ground pepper

3 Tbsp unsalted butter

1 yellow onion, chopped

2 cloves garlic, minced

1 tsp ground cumin

½ tsp ground coriander

4 cups (32 fl oz/1 l) chicken broth

FOR THE SPICY PUMPKIN SEEDS

½ cup (2 oz/60 g) pumpkin seeds, cleaned

1 tsp canola oil

Salt

¼ tsp cayenne pepper

¼ tsp ground cumin

Pinch of ground cinnamon

Preheat the oven to 400°F (200°C) and line a baking sheet with parchment paper. Toss the pumpkin with the oil, season with salt and pepper, and spread on the prepared baking sheet. Roast the pumpkin until soft and caramelized, 30–35 minutes.

In a large, heavy pot, warm the butter over medium-high heat. Add the onion and garlic and sauté until translucent, about 5 minutes. Add the cumin and coriander and cook for 1 minute. Add the broth and pumpkin and bring to a boil. Reduce the heat to low and simmer for 25 minutes. Remove from the heat and let cool slightly.

Working in batches, purée the soup in a blender or food processor. Return to the pot and season with salt and pepper.

To make the spicy pumpkin seeds, lower the oven temperature to 350°F (180°C) and line a baking sheet with parchment paper. In a bowl, toss the seeds with the oil. In another bowl, combine 1 tsp salt, the cayenne, cumin, and cinnamon. Add the pumpkin seeds to the spice mixture and stir to coat. Spread the seeds in a single layer on the prepared baking sheet and bake, stirring once, until golden brown, 10–12 minutes. Serve the soup garnished with the pumpkin seeds.

CELERY ROOT PURÉE WITH CARAMELIZED APPLES

Celery root is just what it sounds like, the root of a variety of celery plant. It's sometimes labeled celeriac. Its subtle flavor stands out best in simple preparations like this one. Make a large batch and freeze extra servings for cold days, but keep the apples separate.

serves 4

2 Tbsp unsalted butter

1 leek, white and pale green parts, chopped

2 celery roots (2 lb/1 kg total), peeled and chopped

3½ cups (28 fl oz/875 ml) vegetable broth

FOR THE CARAMELIZED APPLES

1 Tbsp unsalted butter

1 small Granny Smith apple, peeled, cored, and cut into tiny cubes

¼ tsp dark brown sugar

2 Tbsp half-and-half

Salt and ground white pepper

In a large, heavy pot, warm the butter over medium-high heat. Add the leek and sauté until soft, about 4 minutes. Add the celery roots, stir to coat, and sauté for 2 minutes. Add the broth and bring to a boil. Reduce the heat to low and simmer until the celery root is very tender, 25–30 minutes. Remove from the heat and let cool slightly.

While the soup is cooling, make the caramelized apples. In a frying pan, melt the 1 Tbsp butter over medium-high heat until it foams. Add the apple and sauté for 4 minutes. Sprinkle with the brown sugar, stir to combine, and cook until the apples begin to caramelize, about 3 minutes. Remove from the heat and set aside.

Working in batches, purée the soup in a blender. Return to the pot over medium heat, add the half-and-half, and return just to a gentle boil. Turn off the heat and season with salt and pepper. Serve, garnished with the caramelized apples.

CORN SOUP WITH CHANTERELLES & THYME

Slice the mushrooms crosswise to retain their shape. Chanterelles are beautiful, and you want diners to be able to see that you are serving a really special mushroom. Serve with warm croissants.

serves 4

3 Tbsp unsalted butter

2 Tbsp olive oil

2 shallots, minced

4 cloves garlic, minced

4 cups (32 fl oz/1 l) chicken broth

2 packages (1 lb/500 g each) frozen corn kernels

¼ cup (2 fl oz/60 ml) heavy cream

Salt and freshly ground pepper

2 oz (60 g) chanterelle mushrooms, thinly sliced

½ tsp minced thyme leaves

In a large, heavy pot, warm 2 Tbsp of the butter and the oil over medium-high heat. Add the shallots and garlic and sauté until soft, about 3 minutes. Add the broth and bring to a boil. Add the corn and cook for 5 minutes. Remove from the heat and let cool slightly.

Purée half of the soup in a blender. Return to the pot and stir in the cream. Season with salt and pepper.

In a small frying pan, melt the remaining 1 Tbsp butter over medium-high heat. Add the mushrooms and thyme and sauté, stirring often, until the mushrooms release their liquid and caramelize slightly, about 4 minutes. Serve the soup, garnished with the chanterelles.

SQUASH SOUP WITH SAGE BROWN BUTTER

serves 4–6

1 butternut squash (2 lb/1 kg), peeled and diced

3 Tbsp olive oil

Salt and freshly ground pepper

2 Tbsp unsalted butter

1 yellow onion, chopped

2 cloves garlic, minced

4 cups (32 fl oz/1 l) vegetable broth

FOR THE SAGE BROWN BUTTER

¼ cup (2 oz/60 g) unsalted butter

6 sage leaves

Heavy cream for garnish (optional)

Preheat the oven to 400°F (200°C) and line a baking sheet with parchment paper. Toss the squash with the oil and season with salt and pepper. Place on the prepared baking sheet and roast until tender, about 25 minutes.

In a large, heavy pot, melt the butter over medium-high heat. Add the onion and garlic and sauté until translucent, about 5 minutes. Add the roasted squash and broth and bring to a boil. Reduce the heat to low and simmer for 20 minutes to blend the flavors. Remove from the heat and let cool slightly.

Working in batches, purée the soup in a blender. Return to the pot and season with salt and pepper.

To make the sage brown butter, melt the butter in a small frying pan over low heat. Add the sage leaves and cook until the butter begins to brown and the sage is very aromatic, 3–4 minutes.

Serve the soup, drizzled with the brown butter, 1–2 sage leaves, and a swirl of cream, if desired.

To make the fried shallots, stir together 2 Tbsp all-purpose flour, ½ tsp salt, and ¼ tsp pepper. Add 2 sliced shallots and toss to coat. Heat ½ cup (4 fl oz/ 125 ml) canola oil in a saucepan over medium-high heat until very hot. Shake off any excess flour from the shallots and fry until golden brown, 4 minutes. Drain on paper towels and season with salt.

CHEDDAR & HARD CIDER SOUP WITH FRIED SHALLOTS

serves 6–8

3 Tbsp unsalted butter

2 yellow onions, chopped

1 celery rib, chopped

1 Yukon gold potato, peeled and chopped

2 cloves garlic, minced

2 Tbsp all-purpose flour

2½ cups (20 fl oz/625 ml) chicken broth

2½ cups (20 fl oz/625 ml) hard apple cider

1 cup (8 fl oz/250 ml) half-and-half

2 bay leaves

2 thyme sprigs

2 Tbsp applejack or Calvados brandy

¾ lb (375 g) English Cheddar cheese, shredded

Salt and freshly ground pepper

Fried Shallots *(left)*

In a large, heavy pot, melt the butter over medium-high heat. Add the onions, celery, potato, and garlic and stir. Reduce the heat to low, cover, and cook, stirring occasionally, until the vegetables are softened, about 12 minutes. Sprinkle the flour over the vegetables and cook, stirring constantly, until the flour is incorporated. While stirring constantly, gradually add the broth, cider, and half-and-half. Raise the heat to medium-high, add the bay leaves and thyme sprigs, and bring to a boil. Reduce the heat to low and simmer to blend the flavors, about 10 minutes.

Remove the bay leaves and thyme sprigs from the soup and discard. Remove the soup from the heat and let cool slightly.

Working in batches, purée the soup in a blender. Pour into a clean pot. Stir in the applejack. Off the heat, while whisking constantly, gradually add the cheese one handful at a time. Continue whisking until all the cheese is melted. Place over medium-low heat, stir in 1 tsp salt and pepper to taste, and cook gently, stirring often, until heated through, about 10 minutes.

Taste and adjust the seasoning. Serve, garnished with the fried shallots.

Parsnips and apples are a great flavor pairing: the apples brighten the earthiness of the parsnips. Don't skip the melted Gruyère toasts in this recipe, as dipping them into the soup is a delicious experience.

ROASTED PARSNIP & APPLE PURÉE WITH GRUYÈRE TOASTS

serves 4–6

6 parsnips, peeled and chopped (about 4 cups)

1 Tbsp olive oil

Salt and freshly ground pepper

3 Tbsp unsalted butter

1 small yellow onion, chopped

¼ tsp grated nutmeg

2 Granny Smith apples, peeled, cored, and chopped, plus apple slices for garnish

6 cups (48 fl oz/1.5 l) chicken broth

FOR THE GRUYÈRE TOASTS

4 oz (125 g) Gruyère cheese, shredded

1 loaf crusty bread, cut into slices ¼ inch (6 mm) thick

Preheat the oven to 400°F (200°C). Line a baking sheet with parchment paper. In a bowl, toss the parsnips with the oil and season with salt and pepper. Arrange in a single layer on the prepared pan and roast until beginning to caramelize, 25 minutes.

In a large, heavy pot, melt the butter over medium-high heat. Add the onion and sauté until translucent, about 5 minutes. Add the nutmeg and cook for 1 minute. Add the apples, stir to coat, and cook until they begin to soften, about 5 minutes. Add the broth and parsnips and bring to a boil. Reduce the heat to low and simmer, uncovered, until the parsnips are tender, about 20 minutes. Remove from the heat and let cool slightly.

Working in batches, purée the soup in a blender. Return to the pot and season with salt and pepper.

To make the Gruyère toasts, preheat the broiler to high. Put 2 Tbsp of the grated cheese on each bread slice. Arrange the slices on the baking sheet and broil until the cheese begins to melt, 2–3 minutes.

Serve the soup, garnished with apple slices. Place 1 or 2 Gruyère toasts on the side of each bowl.

To make the sun-dried tomato pesto, in a food processor, mince 1 clove garlic. Coarsely chop and add ½ cup (2½ oz/75 g) drained oil-packed sun-dried tomatoes, 2 Tbsp olive oil, 2 Tbsp finely chopped basil, and 2 Tbsp pine nuts. Season with salt and pepper. Process to form a thick paste, adding more oil if needed.

ROASTED SUMMER VEGETABLE SOUP WITH PESTO

serves 4–6

2 leeks, white and pale green parts, finely chopped

4 carrots, peeled and cut into 2-inch (5-cm) pieces

2 zucchini, cut into 2-inch (5-cm) pieces

2 Asian eggplants, cut into 2-inch (5-cm) pieces

2 large tomatoes, quartered

2 potatoes (about 10 oz/315 g), peeled and cut into 2-inch (5-cm) pieces

4½ cups (36 fl oz/1.1 l) chicken broth, or more as needed

2 Tbsp olive oil

Salt and freshly ground pepper

2 Tbsp finely chopped basil

2 Tbsp fresh lemon juice

Sun-Dried Tomato Pesto *(left)*

Preheat the oven to 425°F (220°C). In a large, heavy roasting pan, combine the leeks, carrots, zucchini, eggplants, tomatoes, and potatoes. Add ½ cup (4 fl oz/125 ml) of the broth and the oil, season with salt and pepper, and mix until the vegetables are well coated. Roast, turning once, until the vegetables are softened, about 40 minutes. Remove from the oven and let cool slightly.

Working in batches, purée the vegetables with ½ cup of the broth. Transfer to a large saucepan and stir in the remaining 3½ cups (28 fl oz/875 ml) broth, the basil, and the lemon juice. If needed, add more broth for the desired consistency. Cook over low heat for 3 minutes to blend the flavors. Season with salt and pepper.

Serve, garnished with pesto.

ROASTED RED PEPPER PURÉE WITH SPICY CORN SALSA

serves 4–6

2 Tbsp olive oil

1 small yellow onion, chopped

2 cloves garlic, minced

1 jar (24 oz/750 g) roasted red bell peppers, drained

1 russet potato, peeled and diced

4 cups (32 fl oz/1 l) chicken broth

1 Tbsp sour cream

Salt and freshly ground pepper

FOR THE SPICY CORN SALSA

1 Tbsp unsalted butter

1 Tbsp minced jalapeño chile

1 Tbsp thinly sliced green onion, white and tender green parts

1 cup (6 oz/185 g) fresh corn kernels (from about 2 ears), or 1 cup frozen corn

Salt and freshly ground pepper

In a large, heavy pot, warm the oil over medium-high heat. Add the onion and garlic and sauté until translucent, about 5 minutes. Add the roasted peppers and potato, stir to coat, and cook for 3 minutes. Add the broth and bring to a boil. Reduce the heat to low and simmer until the potatoes are very tender, 25–30 minutes. Remove from the heat and let cool slightly.

Working in batches, purée the soup in a blender or food processor. Return to the pot, stir in the sour cream, and season with salt and pepper.

Meanwhile, to make the salsa, melt the butter in a small frying pan over high heat. Add the jalapeño and green onion and cook, stirring constantly, until the butter begins to brown, about 2 minutes. Add the corn kernels, stir to combine, and cook for 2 minutes. Season with salt and pepper.

Serve the soup, topped with the corn salsa.

GOLDEN BEET SOUP WITH DILLED GOAT CHEESE

With its distinct caraway nuances and celery-like flavor, feathery dill complements both earthy beets and tangy fresh goat cheese. Golden beets are as sweet as red, but they have a finer, milder taste that lightens this silky soup.

serves 6–8

5 golden beets (about 2½ lb/1.25 kg total), trimmed

1 Yukon gold potato

¼ lb (125 g) fresh goat cheese, crumbled

¾ cup (6 fl oz/180 ml) half-and-half

½ tsp fresh lemon juice

3 Tbsp minced dill, plus leaves for garnish

Salt and freshly ground pepper

2 Tbsp unsalted butter

1 yellow onion, chopped

2 cloves garlic, minced

6 cups (48 fl oz/1.5 l) chicken broth

1 tsp white wine vinegar

Preheat the oven to 400°F (200°C). Wrap the beets and potato in foil and place on a baking sheet. Roast until tender when pierced with a knife, about 1 hour. Open the foil and let cool, then peel and chop the beets and potato.

Meanwhile, in a small bowl, combine the goat cheese, ¼ cup (2 fl oz/60 ml) of the half-and-half, the lemon juice, minced dill, ¼ tsp salt, and pepper to taste. Using a fork, vigorously beat until blended and pourable but still thick. Set aside.

In a large, heavy pot, melt the butter over medium heat. Add the onion and garlic and sauté until softened, about 5 minutes. Add the broth and bring to a boil over medium-high heat. Add the beets and potato, reduce the heat to low, cover partially, and cook for 15 minutes. Remove from the heat and let cool slightly.

Working in batches, purée the soup in a blender. Return to the pot and add the vinegar, 1½ tsp salt, pepper to taste, and the remaining ½ cup (4 fl oz/125 ml) half-and-half and stir. Place over medium-low heat and cook gently, stirring occasionally, until heated through, about 10 minutes.

Season with salt and pepper. Serve, garnished with a dollop of the goat cheese mixture and the dill leaves.

This beautiful spring soup is simply divine, showcasing tender fresh peas. You can substitute frozen peas if necessary, or to enjoy this dish throughout the year. For an elegant and flavorful garnish, swirl crème fraîche or olive oil on top.

PEA & MINT PURÉE WITH LEMON

serves 4–6

2 Tbsp unsalted butter

2 shallots, minced

3 cups (24 fl oz/750 ml) chicken broth

3 cups (15 oz/470 g) fresh or frozen peas, plus more for garnish

½ cup (¾ oz/20 g) chopped mint, plus small leaves for garnish

1 Tbsp sour cream

Grated zest of 1 lemon

Salt and freshly ground pepper

Extra-virgin olive oil for drizzling

In a large, heavy pot, melt the butter over medium-high heat. Add the shallots and cook until soft, 5 minutes. Add the broth and bring to a boil. Add the peas, reserving a few for the garnish, and cook until tender, 3–5 minutes. Stir in the chopped mint. Remove from the heat and let cool slightly.

Working in batches, purée the soup in a blender or food processor. Return to the pot, stir in the sour cream, and warm over medium heat. Turn off the heat and stir in the lemon zest. Season with salt and pepper and serve, garnished with mint leaves and peas and drizzled with oil.

POTATO-LEEK PURÉE WITH SMOKED SALMON & DILL

For a stunning presentation, serve this soup in shallow bowls so the salmon doesn't sink to the bottom. The dill can be replaced by chopped chervil or chives, if you prefer.

serves 6

2 Tbsp olive oil

2 leeks, white and pale green parts, chopped

2 russet potatoes, peeled and finely diced

4 cups (32 fl oz/1 l) chicken broth

½ cup (4 fl oz/125 ml) heavy cream

1 Tbsp chopped dill

Salt and freshly ground pepper

¼ lb (125 g) smoked salmon, chopped

In a large, heavy pot, warm the oil over medium-high heat. Add the leeks and sauté until soft, about 5 minutes. Add the potatoes and the broth and bring to a boil. Reduce the heat to low and simmer until the potatoes are very soft, about 20 minutes. Remove from the heat and let cool slightly.

Working in batches, purée the soup in a blender. Return to the pot and stir in the cream and dill. Return the soup to a gentle boil, turn off the heat, and season with salt and pepper.

Serve, garnished with the smoked salmon.

CARROT & COCONUT PURÉE WITH CURRIED ALMONDS

serves 6–8

1½ tsp sugar

Salt and freshly ground pepper

¼ tsp ground coriander, plus 1 Tbsp

½ tsp curry powder

1½ tsp unsalted butter, plus 3 Tbsp

½ cup (2 oz/60 g) sliced almonds, toasted

1 yellow onion, chopped

2 lb (1 kg) carrots, peeled and thinly sliced

¼ cup (1 oz/30 g) unsweetened shredded coconut, toasted

½ tsp ground ginger

4 cups (32 fl oz/1 l) chicken broth

2 cans (14 oz/440 g each) coconut milk

2 tsp rice vinegar

Stir together ½ tsp of the sugar, ¼ tsp salt, the ¼ tsp coriander, and the curry powder.

In a nonstick frying pan, melt the 1½ tsp butter with 1 Tbsp water and the remaining 1 tsp sugar over medium-high heat. Bring to a boil, swirling the pan to blend. Add the almonds, stir to coat, and cook until the liquid is almost evaporated, about 45 seconds. Transfer to the bowl with the spice mixture and toss to coat the almonds evenly. Pour onto a piece of parchment paper, spread in a single layer, and let cool.

In a large, heavy pot, melt the 3 Tbsp butter over medium-high heat. Add the onion, carrots, coconut, ginger, and the 1 Tbsp coriander and stir to combine. Reduce the heat to low, cover, and cook until the vegetables give off some of their liquid, about 10 minutes. Add the broth, raise the heat to high, and bring to a boil. Reduce the heat to low, cover, and simmer until the carrots are tender, about 20 minutes. Remove from the heat and let cool slightly.

Working in batches, purée the soup in a blender. Pour into a clean pot. Add the coconut milk (reserve some for serving), the vinegar, and 1 tsp salt. Cook gently over medium-low heat, stirring occasionally, until heated through, about 10 minutes. Serve, sprinkled with the spiced almonds and swirled with coconut milk.

To trim a stalk
of asparagus,
gently bend it
about 2 inches
(5 cm) from
the bottom
and the stalk
should snap
naturally, right
at the point
where the tender
and tough parts
meet. Peel any
thicker stems.

CREAM OF ASPARAGUS SOUP

serves 4–6

1 Tbsp unsalted butter

2 Tbsp olive oil

2 leeks, white and light green parts, finely chopped

1 lb (500 g) thick asparagus, trimmed, peeled, and cut into 2-inch (5-cm) pieces, tips reserved

1 russet potato, peeled and cut into 2-inch (5-cm) chunks

4 cups (32 fl oz/1 l) chicken broth

Salt and ground white pepper

Juice of ½ lemon

3 Tbsp crème fraîche or sour cream

1 Tbsp finely chopped chives

In a large, heavy pot, melt the butter with the oil over medium heat. Add the leeks and sauté until softened, about 5 minutes. Add the asparagus stalks and potato and sauté until beginning to soften, about 3 minutes. Add the broth and season with salt and pepper. Bring to a boil over medium-high heat. Reduce the heat to low, cover partially, and cook until the vegetables are very tender, about 15 minutes.

Meanwhile, bring a small saucepan of water to a boil. Add the lemon juice and reserved asparagus tips and cook until crisp-tender, about 3 minutes. Drain and let cool slightly.

Working in batches, purée the soup in a blender. Return to the pot and reheat over low heat. Serve, garnished with the crème fraîche, asparagus tips, and chives.

HEARTY
SOUPS

LEMONY RED LENTIL SOUP WITH FRIED SHALLOTS

An ancient preparation—this is the biblical "mess of pottage" for which Esau sold his birthright—red lentil soup remains common today in Egypt and Lebanon. Red lentils cook more quickly than other varieties, so are ideal for soups and puréeing.

serves 4

2 Tbsp olive oil

1 yellow onion, chopped

1 tsp ground cumin

½ tsp ground coriander

Pinch of red pepper flakes

1 cup (7 oz/220 g) split red lentils, picked over and rinsed

1 carrot, peeled and finely chopped

1 tomato, peeled, seeded, and chopped

4 cups (32 fl oz/1 l) vegetable broth

Salt and freshly ground pepper

Juice of ½ lemon, plus 1 lemon cut into 4 wedges

Fried Shallots (page 82)

In a large, heavy pot, warm the oil over medium-high heat. Add the onion and sauté until soft, about 5 minutes. Add the cumin, coriander, and red pepper flakes and cook, stirring, until the spices are fragrant, about 30 seconds.

Add the lentils, carrot, tomato, and broth. Season with 1 tsp salt and a few grinds of pepper. Bring to a boil, reduce the heat to medium, cover, and simmer until the lentils fall apart and the carrots are soft, about 40 minutes. Remove from the heat and let cool slightly.

Working in batches, purée the soup in a blender. Return to the pot, add the lemon juice, and warm through over medium heat, stirring occasionally.

Serve, garnished with the fried shallots and accompanied with the lemon wedges.

SHORT RIB STEW WITH PAPRIKA SOUR CREAM

Short ribs braise slowly in the oven and come out caramelized and tender. This savory stew uses the shredded meat and the braising liquid. This is a great way to use leftover short rib meat (and if you don't have any leftover braising liquid, you can use beef broth).

serves 4

3 lb (1.5 kg) short ribs, halved

Salt and freshly ground pepper

2 Tbsp olive oil

1 yellow onion, chopped

6 cloves garlic, minced

2 celery ribs, chopped

1 carrot, peeled and chopped

3 cups (24 fl oz/750 ml) dry red wine

2 bay leaves

4½ cups (36 fl oz/1.1 l) beef broth

1 can (15 oz/470 g) cannellini or other white beans, drained

1 can (14½ oz/455 g) diced tomatoes

¼ cup (⅓ oz/10 g) chopped flat-leaf parsley

FOR THE PAPRIKA SOUR CREAM

⅔ cup (5½ oz/170 g) sour cream

1 tsp fresh lemon juice

½ tsp smoked paprika

Salt

Season the short ribs with salt and pepper and refrigerate for at least 6 hours. Remove from the refrigerator, bring to room temperature, and season again with salt and pepper.

Preheat the oven to 350°F (180°C). In a large sauté pan, warm the oil over high heat until very hot. Sear the short ribs until they are browned on all sides, 6–8 minutes, then transfer to a large, heavy ovenproof pot.

Reduce the heat under the sauté pan to medium, add the onion, garlic, celery, and carrot, and sauté for 5 minutes. Add the wine and bay leaves, raise the heat to high, and boil until the liquid has been reduced by half, 10–12 minutes. Add the broth and bring to a boil. Pour the contents of the sauté pan into the pot. Cover tightly, transfer to the oven, and cook for 2½ hours.

Remove the short ribs from the pot and, when they are cool enough to handle, remove the meat from the bones and shred into bite-sized pieces. Strain the braising liquid and reserve 1¼ cups (10 fl oz/310 ml); discard the vegetables left in the strainer.

Put the shredded meat and the reserved braising liquid back into the pot and set over medium heat. Stir in the beans and the tomatoes with their juices and bring to a boil over medium-high heat. Stir in the parsley and season with salt and pepper.

To make the paprika sour cream, in a bowl, stir together the sour cream, lemon juice, paprika, and ¼ tsp salt. Serve the stew, topped with a generous dollop of the paprika sour cream.

ORZO, DELICATA SQUASH & CHICKEN SOUP WITH SAGE

You can save time making this colorful and plentiful soup by using leftover rotisserie or roasted chicken. You can also substitute a different type of squash, or sweet potatoes. Make it meatless by omitting the chicken, substituting vegetable broth, and serving with shaved Parmesan.

serves 4–6

4 delicata squash (2¾ lb/4 kg total), peeled, seeded, and cubed

3 Tbsp olive oil

Salt and freshly ground pepper

2 small skinless, boneless chicken breast halves (about ¾ lb/375 g total)

1 cup (7 oz/220 g) orzo

3 Tbsp unsalted butter

1 small yellow onion, chopped

3 cloves garlic, minced

5 sage leaves, torn into pieces

4 cups (32 fl oz/1 l) chicken broth

Preheat the oven to 400°F (200°C) and line a baking sheet with parchment paper. Toss the squash with 2 Tbsp of the oil, season with salt and pepper, and spread on the prepared baking sheet. Place the chicken on another baking sheet, brush with the remaining 1 Tbsp oil, and season with salt and pepper. Place the squash on the top rack in the oven and the chicken on the lower rack. Roast until the chicken is cooked through and a thermometer inserted into the thickest part reaches 160°F (71°C), about 20 minutes. Remove the chicken from the oven and continue to roast the squash until it is tender and caramelized, about 10 minutes longer. When the chicken is cool enough to handle, shred it into bite-sized pieces.

Put 6 cups (48 fl oz/1.5 l) water in a saucepan over medium-high heat and bring to a boil. Add ½ tsp salt and the orzo and cook for 7 minutes. Drain the pasta and set aside.

In a large, heavy pot over medium-high heat, melt the butter. Add the onion, garlic, and sage and sauté until soft, about 5 minutes. Add the broth and bring to a boil. Add the orzo, shredded chicken, and squash and reduce the heat to low. Simmer for 15 minutes, then season to taste with salt and pepper and serve.

To save time, purchase already-made corn bread. Make sure your pan is really hot when you add the corn bread cubes to ensure that they get a nice golden sear (but work fast so that the butter doesn't burn). Pass extra croutons at the table.

WHITE BEAN & HAM SOUP WITH CORN BREAD CROUTONS

serves 4–6

4 slices thick-cut bacon

½ lb (250 g) cooked ham steak, cubed

1 Tbsp olive oil

1 small yellow onion, diced

3 cloves garlic, minced

2 celery ribs, diced

2 cups (16 fl oz/500 ml) chicken broth

2 cans (15 oz/470 g each) white beans, drained

Salt and freshly ground pepper

FOR THE CORN BREAD CROUTONS

1 Tbsp unsalted butter

1 small loaf corn bread, cut into ½-inch (12-mm) cubes

Set a large, heavy pot over medium-high heat. Add the bacon and cook until crispy, about 8 minutes. Transfer to paper towels to drain. Let cool, then crumble into bite-sized pieces. Set aside in a bowl. Add the ham to the pot and cook, stirring often, until browned, about 4 minutes. Add the ham to the bowl with the bacon.

Add the oil, onion, garlic, and celery to the pot and sauté until the vegetables are soft, about 5 minutes. Add the broth and beans and bring to a boil. Reduce the heat to low and simmer for 10 minutes. Remove from the heat and let cool slightly.

Purée half of the soup in a blender. Return to the pot along with the ham and bacon and stir to combine. Season with salt and pepper.

To make the corn bread croutons, in a frying pan, melt the butter over medium heat. Add the corn bread cubes and cook, turning once, until they are golden brown on both sides.

Serve, topped with the croutons.

SAVORY BARLEY SOUP WITH WILD MUSHROOMS & THYME

Barley, an excellent source of minerals and fiber, deserves its renaissance in the modern kitchen. Thanks to a partial puréeing, this creamy soup supports meaty fall mushrooms. Add a Parmesan rind to the broth as it simmers for a boost in flavor.

serves 4

½ oz (15 g) dried porcini mushrooms

½ cup (4 fl oz/125 ml) dry white wine

1 Tbsp olive oil

½ cup (2 oz/60 g) chopped shallots

2 cloves garlic, minced

8 oz (250 g) cremini mushrooms, chopped

1 tsp minced fresh thyme, or ½ tsp dried

Salt and freshly ground pepper

3 cups (24 fl oz/750 ml) chicken broth

¾ cup (6 oz/185 g) pearl barley

1 Tbsp tomato paste

2 tsp fresh lemon juice

Rinse the porcini well to remove any dirt or grit. In a small saucepan, bring the wine to a simmer. Remove from the heat and add the porcini. Let stand for 15 minutes, then drain the porcini over a bowl, reserving the liquid, and finely chop.

In a large, heavy pot over medium-high heat, warm the oil. Add the shallots and garlic. Sauté until the shallots are wilted, 3–5 minutes. Add the cremini, thyme, ¼ tsp salt, and ¼ tsp pepper. Cook until the cremini release their liquid and begin to brown, 4–5 minutes. Add the reserved mushroom soaking liquid and bring to a boil, scraping up any browned bits from the pan bottom.

Add the broth, barley, tomato paste, 3 cups (24 fl oz/750 ml) water, and the chopped porcini to the pot. Cover and simmer until the barley is tender to the bite, 45–50 minutes. Remove from the heat and let cool slightly.

Purée about 1 cup (8 fl oz/250 ml) of the soup in a blender. Return to the pot, heat until just hot, and stir in the lemon juice. Season with salt and pepper and serve.

Turnips have a delicately sweet flavor when young, but as they mature they lose their sweetness and become woody—so buy them at their peak, between October and February. The greens, which are edible, should be bright green and garden fresh. If unavailable, substitute Swiss chard, dandelion greens, beet greens, or kale.

BEEF STEW WITH TURNIPS & GREENS

serves 6

¼ cup (2 fl oz/60 ml) olive oil

2 yellow onions, finely chopped

2 oz (60 g) bacon or pancetta, finely diced

3 lb (1.5 kg) chuck roast or sirloin tip,
cut into 1–1½-inch (2.5–4-cm) cubes

¼ cup (1½ oz/45 g) all-purpose flour

4 cloves garlic, minced

6 flat-leaf parsley stems, 2 thyme sprigs, and 2 bay leaves
tied together to make a bouquet garni

1½ cups (12 fl oz/375 ml) dry red wine

3 cups (24 fl oz/750 ml) beef broth

1 Tbsp tomato paste

1 bunch turnips with greens, turnips cut into ½-inch (12-mm) chunks
and leaves stemmed and cut crosswise into strips

Salt and freshly ground pepper

In a large, heavy pot, warm the oil over medium heat. Add the onions and bacon and sauté until the onions are soft, about 10 minutes. Transfer to a plate.

Working in batches, add the beef to the pot in a single layer and cook, turning occasionally, until golden brown on all sides, 7–10 minutes. Transfer to a bowl. Return all the meat to the pot, sprinkle with the flour, and cook, stirring, until the meat is evenly coated, about 1 minute. Return the onions and bacon to the pot and add the garlic. Add the bouquet garni to the pot.

Raise the heat to high, pour in the wine, and bring to a boil, stirring to scrape up any browned bits on the bottom of the pot. Reduce the heat to medium and simmer, stirring occasionally, until the liquid is reduced by one-fourth, 3–5 minutes. Stir in the broth and tomato paste. Bring to a boil over high heat, reduce the heat to low, cover, and simmer until the meat is tender, 1½–2 hours.

Remove the bouquet garni and discard. Add the turnips, cover, and cook until tender, about 15 minutes. Add the turnip greens, cover, and cook until wilted, about 2 minutes. Season with salt and pepper and serve.

For the avocado crema, lime juice and sour cream are added to mashed avocados for a smooth, tangy version of guacamole. It melts into this soup, adding a creamy element and also helping to tame the spiciness of the chorizo.

CHORIZO & CHICKEN STEW WITH AVOCADO CREMA

serves 4–6

1 skinless, boneless chicken breast half

½ lb (250 g) Mexican chorizo, cut into slices ½ inch (12 mm) thick

2 Tbsp olive oil

1 yellow onion, chopped

2 cloves garlic, minced

1 red bell pepper, seeded and chopped

4 cups (32 fl oz/1 l) chicken broth

1 Tbsp minced thyme

Salt and freshly ground pepper

FOR THE AVOCADO CREMA

1 avocado, pitted and peeled

¼ cup (2 oz/60 g) sour cream

1 Tbsp fresh lime juice

In a small saucepan, combine the chicken breast with cold water to cover by 1 inch (2.5 cm) and bring to a boil over high heat. Reduce the heat to low and simmer until the chicken is cooked through, 15–18 minutes, skimming off any foam on the surface. Remove the chicken from the pan. When it is cool enough to handle, shred the meat.

Warm a large, heavy pot over medium-high heat. Add the chorizo and cook, stirring often, until browned on both sides, about 8 minutes. Transfer to a bowl. Add the oil and warm over medium-high heat. Add the onion and garlic and sauté until translucent, about 5 minutes. Add the bell pepper, stir to coat, and cook for 3 minutes. Add the shredded chicken, chorizo, broth, and thyme and simmer, uncovered, for about 15 minutes to blend the flavors. Season with salt and pepper.

To make the avocado crema, put the avocado in a small bowl and mash with a fork until creamy and smooth. Add the sour cream, the lime juice, and 2 large pinches of salt and stir to combine.

Serve the soup, accompanied with the avocado crema.

GREEN CHILE STEW

serves 6

3 Tbsp toasted peanut oil or canola oil

2 lb (1 kg) boneless pork shoulder, trimmed and cut into ¾-inch (2-cm) cubes

1 white onion, chopped

2 cloves garlic, minced

½ lb (250 g) white or brown mushrooms, quartered

¾ lb (375 g) small yellow-fleshed potatoes, quartered lengthwise

1½ tsp coriander seeds, toasted and ground

1 tsp dried oregano

2 bay leaves

6 cups (48 fl oz/1.5 l) chicken broth

Salt

12–16 New Mexico green chiles (about 2 lb/1 kg), roasted, peeled, seeded, and chopped

6 Tbsp (3 oz/90 g) sour cream

Cilantro leaves for garnish

In a large, heavy pot, warm the oil over high heat. Working in batches, add the pork and brown well on all sides, 6–8 minutes per batch. Transfer to a plate.

Add the onion to the oil remaining in the pot and sauté over medium-high heat until lightly golden, about 4 minutes. Add the garlic and sauté for 1 minute. Add the mushrooms and sauté until the edges are browned, 3–4 minutes. Add the potatoes, coriander, oregano, and bay leaves and return the meat to the pot. Stir well, pour in the broth, and add 1 tsp salt. Bring to a boil, reduce the heat to medium, and simmer, uncovered, until the meat is just tender, about 30 minutes.

Add the chiles and simmer, uncovered, until the meat is very tender, about 20 minutes. Stir in another 1 tsp salt, then taste and adjust with more salt if necessary. Serve, garnished with the sour cream and cilantro.

This rich, lemony chicken-and-rice soup is a signature dish of Greece. To help prevent the eggs from curdling, they must be tempered by whisking a small amount of hot liquid into the yolks to heat them slightly before adding them to the hot mixture.

AVGOLEMONO

serves 4

6 cups (48 fl oz/1.5 l) chicken broth

½ cup (3½ oz/105 g) long-grain white rice

4 egg yolks, lightly beaten

¼ cup (2 fl oz/60 ml) fresh lemon juice

1 tsp finely chopped lemon zest

Salt and ground white pepper

2 Tbsp finely chopped flat-leaf parsley

In a large, heavy pot, bring the broth to a boil over medium-high heat. Add the rice and cook, uncovered, until tender, about 15 minutes.

In a bowl, whisk together the egg yolks, lemon juice, and lemon zest. Whisking constantly, slowly pour 1 cup (8 fl oz/250 ml) of the hot broth into the egg mixture. Reduce the heat under the broth to medium-low and slowly stir the egg mixture into the pot. Cook, stirring, until the soup is slightly thickened, 3–4 minutes. Do not let it boil.

Season with salt and pepper and serve, garnished with the parsley.

SWEET ONION SOUP WITH BLUE CHEESE TOASTS

Vidalia onions have a high sugar content and caramelize beautifully. But they really do take 30 minutes to reach their optimal flavor, so be patient at the stove.

serves 4–6

3 Tbsp unsalted butter

2 Tbsp olive oil

4 sweet onions, such as Vidalia, thinly sliced

1 Tbsp balsamic vinegar

3 cloves garlic, minced

¼ cup (2 fl oz/60 ml) dry white wine

3 cups (24 fl oz/750 ml) chicken broth

Salt and freshly ground pepper

FOR THE BLUE CHEESE TOASTS

1 baguette, cut into 8–12 thin slices

3 oz (90 g) blue cheese, crumbled

In a large, heavy pot, melt the butter with the oil over high heat. Add the onions and sauté until they begin to soften, 5–7 minutes. Reduce the heat to low and continue to cook, stirring occasionally, for 30 minutes. Add the vinegar, stir to combine, and cook, stirring occasionally, for 30 minutes. Stir in the garlic and cook for 5 minutes. Add the wine and cook for 2 minutes. Add the broth, raise the heat to medium-high, and bring to a boil. Remove from the heat and let cool slightly.

Purée half of the soup in a blender. Return to the pot and season with salt and pepper.

Meanwhile, to make the blue cheese toasts, preheat the broiler to high. Place the bread slices on a baking sheet and cover each with blue cheese. Place under the broiler until the cheese is melted and the bread is toasted, 1–2 minutes.

Serve, topping each bowl with 2 or 3 toasts.

KIELBASA & SAUERKRAUT SOUP

Germany is to thank for this genius combination of sausages and pickled cabbage, a sour-savory comfort food. This soup feeds a crowd, but it also freezes well if you have any left over. Serve with hunks of freshly baked pumpernickel or rye bread.

serves 8–10

1 lb (500 g) kielbasa sausage, sliced

2 Tbsp olive oil

2 yellow onions, thinly sliced

4 cloves garlic, minced

1 sweet potato (about 10 oz/315 g), peeled and shredded

6 cups (48 fl oz/1.5 l) chicken broth

1 lb (500 g) sauerkraut, drained

2 Tbsp tomato paste

Salt and freshly ground pepper

Warm a large, heavy pot over medium-high heat. Add the kielbasa slices and sauté until browned on both sides, about 8 minutes. Transfer to a bowl and set aside.

Put the oil in the same pot. Add the onions and garlic and cook, stirring often and scraping up the brown bits on the bottom of the pot, until softened, 5–7 minutes. Add the sweet potato, the broth, and 1 cup (8 fl oz/250 ml) water and bring to a boil. Reduce the heat to low and simmer, uncovered, for 10 minutes. Add the sauerkraut, tomato paste, and kielbasa, stir well to combine, and simmer, uncovered, for 10 minutes. Season with salt and pepper and serve.

LAMB & DRIED APRICOT STEW

This aromatic stew is even better the next day, once the spices have had time to really infuse the meat with flavor. Serve with a simple green salad dressed with a lemony vinaigrette.

serves 6–8

2 Tbsp olive oil

1½ lb (750 g) boneless lamb shoulder, trimmed and cut into 1-inch (2.5-cm) cubes

1 large yellow onion, chopped

3 cloves garlic, minced

2 tsp ground cumin

½ tsp ground coriander

¼ tsp cayenne pepper

Salt and freshly ground black pepper

2 cups (16 fl oz/500 ml) chicken broth

1 can (14½ oz/455 g) diced tomatoes

1 can (8¾ oz/270 g) chickpeas, rinsed

¼ cup (2 oz/60 g) dried apricots, halved

1 cinnamon stick

3 Tbsp chopped flat-leaf parsley

In a large, heavy pot, warm the oil over medium-high heat. Cook the lamb in 2 batches until browned on all sides, 6–8 minutes per batch. Transfer to a bowl.

Add the onion and garlic and sauté until soft, 5–7 minutes. Add the cumin, coriander, and cayenne, season with ¼ tsp black pepper, and cook, stirring constantly, for 2 minutes. Add the broth and bring to a simmer, stirring to scrape up any browned bits on the bottom of the pot. Add the tomatoes, chickpeas, apricots, cinnamon stick, and lamb and bring to a boil. Reduce the heat to low, cover partially, and simmer, stirring occasionally, until the lamb is tender and the stew thickens, about 1¼ hours.

Stir in the parsley, season with salt and pepper, and serve.

Tone down the spice in this soup by using half spicy and half sweet or all sweet Italian sausage. Serve with warm garlic bread.

SPICY SAUSAGE & BROCCOLI RABE SOUP

serves 4–6

1 lb (500 g) spicy Italian sausages

2 Tbsp olive oil

1 large yellow onion, chopped

5 cloves garlic, thinly sliced

6 cups (48 fl oz/1.5 l) chicken broth

½ bunch broccoli rabe, tough stems peeled, cut into ¾-inch (2-cm) pieces

2 Tbsp tomato paste

Salt and freshly ground pepper

Grated pecorino cheese for serving

In a frying pan, cook the sausages over medium heat, turning occasionally, until golden brown and cooked all the way through, about 15 minutes. Let cool, then cut into slices ¼ inch (6 mm) thick. Set aside.

In a large, heavy pot, warm the oil over medium-high heat. Add the onion and garlic and sauté until translucent, about 5 minutes. Add the broth and bring to a boil. Add the broccoli rabe, tomato paste, and sliced sausage, adjust the heat to maintain a simmer, and cook, uncovered, until the broccoli rabe is tender, 7–8 minutes. Season with salt and pepper and serve, topped with grated cheese.

CRANBERRY BEAN & PAPPARDELLE SOUP

Many Italian soups feature a combination of beans and pasta. Red-speckled cranberry beans, an Italian favorite (also called borlotti beans), are worth seeking out if you've never tried them, although other types of cooked beans can be substituted here.

serves 8

1½ oz (45 g) dried porcini mushrooms, soaked in hot water to cover for 30 minutes

8 Tbsp (4 fl oz/125 ml) olive oil

1 clove garlic, minced

Small handful of sage leaves, finely chopped, plus torn whole leaves for garnish

1 cup (8 fl oz/250 ml) canned diced tomatoes, with juices

8 cups (64 fl oz/2 l) chicken broth

1 cup (3 oz/90 g) roughly broken pappardelle or tagliatelle

1 can (15 oz/470 g) cranberry (borlotti) beans, drained

Salt and freshly ground pepper

Drain the mushrooms, rinsing if they are gritty, then squeeze out the excess moisture. In a large, heavy pot, warm 3 Tbsp of the oil over medium heat. Add the garlic, chopped sage, and mushrooms and sauté for 3 minutes. Add the tomatoes and cook, stirring occasionally, until the flavors are well blended, about 5 minutes.

Pour in the broth and bring to a boil. Add the pasta and cook, uncovered, for 5 minutes. Reduce the heat to medium. Stir in the beans. Season with salt and pepper and serve, garnished with the torn sage leaves and drizzled with the remaining 5 Tbsp (3 fl oz/80 ml) oil.

BARLEY-LEEK SOUP WITH MINI CHICKEN MEATBALLS

serves 8–10

This is a great soup to make with kids, who will have fun forming the meatballs and love eating the end result. The meatballs are also delicious served with pasta or couscous. The meatballs can be made ahead and frozen.

1 Tbsp unsalted butter

2 Tbsp olive oil

3 leeks, white and pale green parts, chopped

3 cloves garlic, minced

½ lb (250 g) cremini mushrooms, sliced

2 Tbsp tomato paste

¼ cup (2 fl oz/60 ml) dry white wine

2 cups (12 oz/375 g) pearl barley

8 cups (64 fl oz/2 l) chicken broth, plus more as needed

FOR THE MEATBALLS

Oil for greasing

1 lb (500 g) ground chicken

½ cup (2 oz/60 g) grated Parmesan cheese

¼ cup (1 oz/30 g) plain dried bread crumbs

2 Tbsp minced flat-leaf parsley, plus ½ cup (¾ oz/20 g) chopped parsley for garnish

1 Tbsp tomato paste

Salt and freshly ground pepper

In a large, heavy pot, melt the butter with the oil over medium-high heat. Add the leeks and garlic and sauté until very soft, about 5 minutes. Add the mushrooms and cook, stirring often, until they begin to soften, about 5 minutes. Add the tomato paste and wine, stir to combine, and cook for 4 minutes. Add the barley and 8 cups broth and bring to a boil. Reduce the heat to low, cover, and simmer until the barley is tender, about 45 minutes.

Meanwhile, to make the meatballs, preheat the oven to 375°F (190°C). Oil a baking sheet. In a bowl, combine the chicken, Parmesan, bread crumbs, 2 Tbsp parsley, and tomato paste. Add 1 tsp salt and ½ tsp pepper and stir to combine. The mixture will be very sticky. To form the meatballs, use two small spoons to scoop up the mixture and transfer it to the prepared sheet. Bake until the meatballs are cooked through and no longer pink in the center, 10–12 minutes.

Add the meatballs to the soup and stir in gently. If the soup is too thick, add more broth and heat through. Season with salt and pepper and serve, garnished with the ½ cup chopped parsley.

Long, slow simmering gives this Texas-style chili time to develop a complex, robust flavor and hearty texture. You can garnish the chili with just about anything you like, from sour cream to chopped onions to shredded cheese.

CHILI CON CARNE

serves 4–6

2 lb (1 kg) boneless beef chuck, trimmed and cut into ½-inch (12-mm) cubes

Salt and freshly ground pepper

2 Tbsp canola oil

½ cup (2 oz/60 g) finely chopped mixed chiles, such as jalapeño, serrano, and poblano, seeded if desired

1 small red bell pepper, seeded and finely chopped

8 cloves garlic, minced

4 tsp chili powder

1 tsp ground cumin

½ tsp ground coriander

1 can (28 oz/875 g) diced tomatoes

1 tsp dried oregano

2 cups (16 fl oz/500 ml) beef broth or water

1 cup (8 oz/250 g) sour cream (optional)

Leaves from 12 cilantro sprigs

Sprinkle the meat evenly with salt and pepper. In a large, heavy frying pan, warm 1 Tbsp of the oil over medium heat. Working in batches, brown the beef cubes on all sides, about 5 minutes per batch. Transfer to a large, heavy pot.

Warm the remaining 1 Tbsp oil in the pan over medium heat. Add the chiles, bell pepper, and garlic and sauté until the vegetables are softened and beginning to turn golden, about 5 minutes. Stir in the chili powder, cumin, and coriander and cook for about 1 minute. Add the tomatoes with their juices and the oregano, season with salt and pepper, and stir well to scrape up any browned bits on the pan bottom.

Add the vegetable mixture to the pot with the beef. Place over medium heat, add the broth, and bring to a gentle boil, stirring occasionally. Reduce the heat to maintain a gentle simmer, cover, and cook until the meat is very tender and the liquid is slightly thickened, about 2½ hours. If the chili seems too soupy, uncover the pot for the last 30 minutes to evaporate some of the liquid.

Season the chili with salt and pepper and serve, garnished with sour cream, if desired, and cilantro leaves.

FINE
SOUPS

Here's a fresh take on a classic chowder, made with flavorful smoked fish. For a lighter version, use whole milk in place of the cream.

SMOKED TROUT CHOWDER

serves 4–6

3 Tbsp unsalted butter

1 yellow onion, chopped

1 fennel bulb (¾ lb/375 g), stalks and fronds removed, quartered, cored, and thinly sliced

2 cups (16 fl oz/500 ml) chicken broth

1 cup (8 fl oz/250 ml) bottled clam juice

3 small red potatoes, cut into small dice

1 cup (8 fl oz/250 ml) heavy cream

8 oz (250 g) smoked trout, crumbled

2 tsp fresh lemon juice

1 Tbsp minced dill

Salt and freshly ground pepper

In a large, heavy pot, melt the butter over medium-high heat. Add the onion and fennel and sauté until soft, about 7 minutes. Add the broth and clam juice and bring to a boil. Add the potatoes, reduce the heat to medium-low, and simmer until the potatoes are tender, about 8 minutes. Add the cream, smoked trout, lemon juice, and dill and cook for 4 minutes. Season with salt and pepper and serve.

SUN-DRIED TOMATO SOUP WITH CRAB

Sun-dried tomatoes give this soup a stunning, deep red color and complex flavor. The crab garnish gives it a luxurious and indulgent feel, but you could easily substitute cooked shrimp or even herbed croutons.

serves 4

2 Tbsp unsalted butter

2 shallots, minced

1 cup (5 oz/150 g) drained oil-packed sun-dried tomatoes, julienned

1 can (15 oz/470 g) diced tomatoes

1½ cups (12 fl oz/375 ml) chicken broth

3 Tbsp heavy cream

Salt and freshly ground pepper

¼ lb (125 g) fresh lump crabmeat, picked over for shell fragments

2 Tbsp chopped chives

In a large saucepan, melt the butter over medium-high heat. Add the shallots and sauté until soft, about 5 minutes. Add the sun-dried tomatoes, diced tomatoes, and broth and bring to a boil. Reduce the heat to low and simmer for 20 minutes. Remove from the heat and let cool slightly.

Working in batches, purée the soup in a blender or food processor. Return to the saucepan over low heat and add the cream. Stir to combine, season with salt and pepper, and serve, topped with the crabmeat and sprinkled with the chives.

A traditional holiday food, oysters are at their best during the winter months in most climates. If you live in an area where oysters are plentiful, you can shuck your own or buy freshly shucked; you will need about 36 oysters in the shell. If not, or if you are short on time, use those sold in glass jars at fish and butcher shops.

OYSTER STEW WITH ROSEMARY

serves 8–10

1 Tbsp unsalted butter

1 Tbsp canola oil

1 small yellow onion, finely chopped

2 celery ribs, finely chopped

¼ cup (2 fl oz/60 ml) dry white wine or vermouth

6 cups (48 fl oz/1.5 l) chicken broth

Salt and ground white pepper

1 cup (8 fl oz/250 ml) half-and-half or cream

3 pints (3 lb/1.5 kg) shucked oysters with their liquor

1 Tbsp minced rosemary, plus more for garnish

In a large, heavy pot, melt the butter with the oil over medium heat. Add the onion and celery and sauté until the onion is translucent, about 3 minutes. Add the wine and cook, stirring occasionally, for 3–4 minutes. Add the broth and season with salt and pepper to taste. Reduce the heat to low, cover, and simmer for 5 minutes.

Stir the half-and-half into the broth mixture and simmer, uncovered, for 5 minutes. Add the oysters and their liquor and simmer, uncovered, until the oysters have plumped up and their edges are curled, about 3 minutes. Stir in the 1 Tbsp rosemary. Season with salt and pepper and serve, garnished with the remaining rosemary.

SAFFRON FREGOLA WITH SEAFOOD

A bit of culinary exotica, fregola is a type of pasta from the Italian island of Sardinia. The more common Israeli couscous may be substituted. Serve this hearty stew with a refreshing butter lettuce and pear salad and plenty of crusty bread for dipping.

serves 4

1 tsp saffron threads

¼ cup (2 fl oz/60 ml) dry white wine

2 Tbsp olive oil

½ lb (250 g) medium shrimp, shelled and deveined

½ lb (250 g) medium scallops, tough muscles removed

1 small yellow onion, chopped

2 cloves garlic, minced

2 cups (16 fl oz/500 ml) chicken broth

1 cup (6 oz/185 g) fregola (Sardinian couscous) or Israeli couscous

Salt and freshly ground pepper

½ lb (250 g) clams, scrubbed

2 Tbsp minced flat-leaf parsley

Crush the saffron in a bowl and add the white wine. Set aside.

In a large, heavy pot, warm 1 Tbsp of the oil over high heat. When the pan is very hot, add the shrimp and sear for 1 minute on each side (do not cook all the way through). Transfer to a bowl. Add the scallops and sear for 1 minute on each side, also without cooking all the way through. Transfer to the bowl with the shrimp.

Add the remaining 1 Tbsp oil, onion, and garlic to the same pot and sauté until soft, about 5 minutes. Add the saffron mixture and cook for 2 minutes. Add the broth and bring to a boil. Add the fregola, stir to combine, and reduce the heat to medium-low. Cook for 12 minutes. Season with salt and pepper.

Add the clams, discarding any that do not close to the touch. Cover the saucepan tightly and steam for 3 minutes. Remove the lid and quickly add the shrimp and scallops. Tightly cover the saucepan again and continue to cook just until the clams open and the shrimp and scallops are cooked through, about 3 minutes. Discard any unopened clams. Serve, sprinkled with the parsley.

For this soup, you can substitute bay scallops, which are smaller, but cut the searing time in half. Shrimp or calamari are also good options. For a creamy version, stir in ½ cup (4 fl oz/ 125 ml) heavy cream after reducing the heat to low and before seasoning with salt and pepper.

SCALLOPS & PANCETTA IN SAFFRON BROTH

serves 4

Large pinch of saffron threads

½ cup (4 fl oz/125 ml) dry white wine

3 oz (90 g) sliced pancetta, diced

2 Tbsp unsalted butter

2 shallots, finely chopped

½ cup (4 fl oz/125 ml) dry sherry

3 cups (24 fl oz/750 ml) chicken broth

Salt and freshly ground black pepper

12 large sea scallops (about 1¼ lb/625 total), tough muscles removed

2 Tbsp olive oil

1 Tbsp chopped chervil or parsley

Using your fingers, gently crush the saffron into a small bowl and add the white wine. Set aside.

In a large, heavy pot, cook the pancetta over medium-high heat, stirring often, until golden, about 4 minutes. Transfer to paper towels to drain. Set aside.

Add the butter and shallots to the pot and sauté until soft, about 5 minutes. Add the sherry and cook until the liquid evaporates, about 4 minutes. Add the saffron-wine mixture and cook until the liquid is reduced by half. Add the broth and bring to a boil. Reduce the heat to low and season with salt and pepper.

Warm a frying pan over high heat. Toss the scallops with the oil and season with salt and pepper. When the frying pan is very hot, add the scallops and sear on one side until lightly browned, 2–3 minutes. Flip the scallops and cook until lightly browned on the other side, 1–2 minutes.

Ladle the broth into shallow bowls. Place 3 scallops in each bowl, sprinkle with the reserved pancetta and chervil, and serve.

CHICKEN SOUP WITH GNOCCHI, BASIL & PARMESAN

serves 4–6

2 small skinless, boneless chicken breast halves

3 Tbsp olive oil

Salt and freshly ground pepper

½ small yellow onion, chopped

2 garlic cloves, minced

4 cups chicken broth

1 can (14½ oz/455 g) oz) diced tomatoes

1 package (17½ oz/545 g) potato gnocchi

1 cup (1 oz/30 g) baby spinach

¼ cup (⅓ oz/10 g) chopped basil

Grated Parmesan cheese for serving

Preheat the oven to 375°F (190°C). Place the chicken breasts on a baking sheet, brush with 1 Tbsp of the oil, and season with salt and pepper. Roast the chicken until opaque throughout, 18–20 minutes. Let the chicken cool to the touch, then shred into bite-sized pieces.

In a large, heavy pot, warm the remaining 2 Tbsp oil over medium-high heat. Add the onion and garlic and sauté until translucent, about 5 minutes. Add the broth and tomatoes with their juices and bring to a boil. Add the chicken and gnocchi and cook for 5 minutes. Remove from the heat, add the spinach and basil, and stir just until wilted. Season with salt and pepper.

Serve, passing the Parmesan at the table.

MISO SOUP WITH BLACK COD & GREEN ONIONS

This beautiful soup makes a perfect light dinner on a warm summer evening. Serve it in shallow bowls to showcase the caramelized black cod. A cold seaweed or sesame-spinach salad would pair well.

serves 2

1 piece kombu, about 3 inches (7.5 cm)

½ cup (½ oz/15 g) bonito flakes

2 Tbsp white miso paste

5 oz (155 g) black cod, cut into 2–4 pieces

1 Tbsp olive oil

Salt and freshly ground pepper

1 green onion, white and tender green parts, thinly sliced

Put 3 cups (24 fl oz/750 ml) cold water and the kombu in a saucepan over medium heat. Bring to a boil and then remove and discard the kombu. Turn off the heat, add the bonito flakes, stir gently once, and let sit for 5 minutes. Strain the soup through a fine-mesh sieve and return the broth to the saucepan.

Put the miso paste in a small bowl and add ¼ cup (2 fl oz/60 ml) of the warm broth. Stir until the mixture is very smooth. Add the miso mixture to the saucepan and warm gently, taking care not to let the soup come to a boil.

Place a small frying pan over high heat until it is very hot. Season the cod with the oil, salt, and pepper and sear until just cooked through, 4 minutes per side.

To serve, ladle the soup into bowls, top with one or two pieces of fish, and sprinkle with green onions.

To make bruschetta, brush both sides of 4 thick slices of crusty Italian bread with olive oil and rub with the cut side of a garlic clove. Warm a grill pan over high heat until very hot. Add the bread and grill until toasted with grill marks, about 3 minutes per side.

LUMP CRAB IN TOMATO-ROSEMARY BROTH

serves 4

2 lb (1 kg) ripe plum tomatoes, halved

4 Tbsp olive oil

Salt and freshly ground pepper

2 shallots, minced

5 cloves garlic, minced

½ tsp red pepper flakes

½ cup (4 fl oz/125 ml) dry white wine

4 tsp rosemary leaves, chopped

2 cups (16 fl oz/500 ml) chicken broth

1 Tbsp unsalted butter

¼ lb (125 g) fresh lump crabmeat, picked over for shell fragments

Bruschetta *(left)*

Preheat the oven to 450°F (230°C). Arrange the tomatoes, cut side up, in a single layer on a baking sheet, drizzle with 2 Tbsp of the oil, and season with salt and pepper. Roast the tomatoes until very soft and caramelized, 25–30 minutes. Set aside.

In a large, heavy pot, warm the remaining 2 Tbsp oil over medium heat. Add the shallots and garlic and sauté for 2 minutes. Add the red pepper flakes and cook for 1 minute. Add the tomatoes with all their juices and the white wine and simmer for 3 minutes. Add the rosemary and broth and bring to a boil. Reduce the heat to low and simmer for 15 minutes. Season with salt and pepper. For a clear broth, strain through a fine-mesh sieve into a medium saucepan set over low heat.

In a small frying pan, melt the butter over high heat until sizzling. Add the crabmeat, stir gently to coat, and heat for 30 seconds.

Ladle the soup into bowls, pile the crabmeat in the middle of each bowl, and serve with pieces of bruschetta alongside.

You can use cockles or mussels in place of the clams in this recipe. Serve with crusty country-style bread to soak up the broth. The parsley vinaigrette is also delicious drizzled on sliced grilled chicken or fish.

CLAMS IN FENNEL BROTH WITH PARSLEY VINAIGRETTE

serves 4

FOR THE VINAIGRETTE

⅓ cup (½ oz/15 g) minced flat-leaf parsley

Grated zest and juice of 1 lemon

1 Tbsp extra-virgin olive oil

1 Tbsp Dijon mustard

1 clove garlic, minced

Salt and freshly ground pepper

1 Tbsp unsalted butter

1 Tbsp olive oil

2 cloves garlic, sliced

2 small fennel bulbs, including stalks and fronds, sliced

2 shallots, minced

½ cup (4 fl oz/125 ml) dry white wine

1 cup (8 fl oz/250 ml) chicken broth

2 lb (1 kg) manila clams, scrubbed

To make the vinaigrette, in a small bowl, stir together the parsley, lemon zest and juice, oil, mustard, and garlic. Season with salt and pepper and let stand at room temperature.

In a large, heavy pot, melt the butter with the oil over medium-high heat. Add the garlic, fennel, and shallots and sauté until soft, about 5 minutes. Add the wine and cook for 2 minutes. Add the broth and bring to a boil. Add the clams to the pot, discarding any that do not close to the touch. Cover and cook until the clams open, 6–8 minutes. Discard any unopened clams.

Ladle the clams and broth into bowls, drizzle with the vinaigrette, and serve.

A perfect spring luncheon soup, this is wonderful served with a glass of dry white wine or even Champagne. You can make the soup a day ahead and reheat it gently while you fry the prosciutto and poach the eggs. Serve with toasted baguette slices.

ASPARAGUS SOUP WITH POACHED EGGS & CRISPY PROSCIUTTO

serves 4

2 oz (60 g) prosciutto, thinly sliced

2 Tbsp unsalted butter

1 yellow onion, chopped

2 cloves garlic, minced

¼ cup (2 fl oz/60 ml) dry white wine

3 cups (24 fl oz/750 ml) chicken broth

2 bunches asparagus, trimmed and cut into ½-inch (12-mm) pieces

2 Tbsp heavy cream

Salt and freshly ground pepper

1 tsp white vinegar

4 eggs

Lay the prosciutto slices in the bottom of a large, heavy pot. Cook over medium-high heat, turning with tongs, until the prosciutto is crispy, about 7 minutes. Transfer to paper towels. Let cool, then crumble.

Add the butter, onion, and garlic to the same pot and sauté until translucent, 5 minutes. Add the wine, bring to a simmer, stir to scrape up any browned bits on the bottom of the pot, and cook for 3 minutes. Add the broth and bring to a boil. Add the asparagus and cook, uncovered, until tender, 8–10 minutes. Remove from the heat and let cool slightly.

Working in batches, purée the soup in a blender. Return to the pot, add the cream, and bring to a boil over medium heat. Season with salt and pepper and keep warm over low heat.

In a frying pan, heat 1 inch (2.5 cm) of water over medium heat. Add the vinegar and reduce the heat to keep the water at a gentle simmer. Break an egg into a small bowl and, using a large spoon, place the egg gently in the water. Using a tablespoon, occasionally spoon the hot water over the top of the exposed egg. Cook until the egg is set but the yolk is still runny, about 5 minutes. Remove the egg with a slotted spoon. Repeat to poach the remaining eggs.

Ladle the soup into bowls, top with the poached eggs and prosciutto, and serve.

This simple recipe
can be made
even easier by
using shredded
rotisserie or
grilled chicken.
Adding the rind
from a piece of
Parmesan cheese
during cooking
adds depth of
flavor to a soup.

PARMESAN BROTH WITH LEMON, CHICKEN & SPINACH

serves 4–6

2 small skinless, boneless chicken breast halves (about ¾ lb/375 g)

2 Tbsp olive oil

1 small yellow onion, chopped

3 cloves garlic, minced

1-inch (2.5-cm) piece of Parmesan cheese rind,
plus cheese shavings for garnish

6 cups (48 fl oz/1.5 l) chicken broth

Juice of 1 lemon

1 small bunch spinach, tough stems removed

Salt and freshly ground pepper

In a small saucepan, combine the chicken breasts with cold water to cover by 1 inch (2.5 cm). Bring to a boil over medium-high heat. Reduce the heat to low and simmer until the chicken is opaque throughout, 15–18 minutes, skimming off any foam on the surface. Transfer to a plate and let cool. Shred the chicken.

In a large, heavy pot, warm the oil over medium-high heat. Add the onion and garlic and cook until translucent, about 5 minutes. Add the Parmesan rind, broth, and lemon juice and bring to a boil. Reduce the heat to low and simmer, uncovered, for 15 minutes. Add the spinach and chicken and continue to simmer, stirring constantly, just until the spinach is wilted. Remove and discard the Parmesan rind and season with salt and pepper. Serve, topped with Parmesan shavings.

TOMATO BROTH WITH SHRIMP, FETA & OREGANO

This simple tomato soup, adorned with a trio of classic Greek ingredients— shrimp, feta cheese, and oregano—comes together in less than 30 minutes. Serve with sliced country bread that's been lightly toasted and rubbed with a cut garlic clove.

serves 4–6

2 Tbsp olive oil

1 small yellow onion, chopped

4 cloves garlic, minced

3 cans (14½ oz/455 g each) diced tomatoes, drained

4 cups (32 fl oz/1 l) chicken broth

Salt and freshly ground pepper

½ lb (250 g) medium shrimp, peeled and deveined

½ lb (250 g) feta cheese, crumbled

2 Tbsp chopped oregano

In a large, heavy pot, warm the oil over medium-high heat. Add the onion and garlic and sauté until translucent, 5–7 minutes. Add the tomatoes and sauté for 4 minutes. Add the broth and bring to a boil. Reduce the heat to low and simmer for 20 minutes. Remove from the heat and let cool slightly.

Purée half of the soup in a blender. Return to the pot and season with salt and pepper. Keep warm over low heat while you prepare the shrimp.

Preheat the broiler to high. Pour ½ cup (4 fl oz/125 ml) of the tomato broth into a shallow oven-safe dish. Lay the shrimp in a single layer on top of the tomato broth and sprinkle with the feta. Put the shrimp under the broiler for 4 minutes. Remove the shrimp, sprinkle with the oregano, and put back under the broiler until cooked through, 1–2 minutes. Ladle the broth into bowls, top each serving with the shrimp and feta, and serve.